MW00475777

ASSESSMENT OF GIFTEDNESS

A Concise and Practical Guide

SECOND EDITION

Julie Lamb Milligan, Ph.D.
Arkansas State University

YBK Publishers
New York

YBK Publishers, Inc.
39 Crosby St.
New York, NY 10013
www.ybkpublishers.com

ISBN 978-0-9824012-9-3

Library of Congress Control Number: 2010932288

Manufactured in the United States of America

Ver 08-10

Contents

Tables

Figures

Preface

In most university graduate programs across the United States, the preparation of teachers of gifted children includes several topics related to giftedness. These topics are: (a) characteristics of giftedness, (b) curriculum, (c) program development, (d) affective issues, (e) creativity, and (f) assessment. There are many exceptional textbooks to guide a course of study in almost any topic related to giftedness.

Yet, as a professor of gifted, talented and creative education, each time I prepared to teach ELSE 5733 Assessment for Gifted, Talented, & Creative, I found limited resources which addressed the assessment of giftedness. The idea for this book emerged from my own feelings of need based on the lack of a concise text I could use in class.

I thought back to the days when I was a young graduate student learning the 'ins and outs' of identifying giftedness through an understanding of assessment instruments, assessment procedures, and the overall identification process. It was important to know about identification procedures appropriate for all school-age students including students at the primary level, those from diverse populations, and the link between identification and program services. Reflectively and based on my lack of expertise at that beginning stage, in 2007 I prepared a text that I hoped would be beneficial to the novice toward better understanding the assessment and identification process or for educators of gifted students who were establishing or refurbishing identification procedures. In this 2nd edition of *Assessment of Giftedness: A Concise and Practical Guide*, research since that time has been included. Additional resources have been included regarding test instruments and web resources.

Thanks to my husband, Keith, and our children, Micahel-Jayce and Libby, who are always supportive of my professional endeavors, I have been able to accomplish this task at home. I could not ask for a more conducive household in which to express my ideas and work on educational projects.

Acknowledgment is also extended to Tim Coone, who assisted with editing and preparing the index. I owe much gratitude to Tim.

This book is dedicated to

Debbie Beineke

who began her master's degree in gifted, talented, and creative education by taking the ELSE 5733 Assessment course. Just after she completed the course, she was diagnosed with ovarian cancer. Debbie lost her battle with the disease before having the opportunity to take additional coursework and achieve her degree. But for years, she had been a dedicated classroom teacher who was most devoted to students from diverse cultural backgrounds and those with diverse learning needs. May God bless Debbie eternally for the positive impact she had on the lives of multitudes of students.

Chapter I

History of Assessing and Identifying Giftedness

The Earliest Definitions of "High IQ" and "Giftedness"

What is IQ, and how did high IQ and giftedness become synonymous? Before the development of IQ measures, the British psychologist Francis Galton (1869) began the quest for answers pertaining to mental superiority by examining the achievements of individuals. Galton (whose research was very subjective and moralistic and whose primary interest was in the inheritability of such traits) devised a normal curve for personal accomplishments by individuals of his day. Those who deviated from the mean on the upper end, about 1 percent of the total population, such as judges and bishops, were considered inspired, mentally superior individuals.

In 1904, the French psychologist Alfred Binet, still often called the father of intelligence testing, was commissioned by the French government to develop a test instrument that would identify slow learners. He and a colleague, Theophile Simon, created a series of questions or problems related to skills to determine intellectual abilities such as *attention, perception, memory,* _reasoning_, and _verbal comprehension_ (Binet, 1905; Kite, 1916). These problems were given to school-age children of France. The questions that did not discriminate between "dull" and "normal" children were eliminated (Wolf, 1973). With refinement, Binet and Simon developed a test that sampled several cognitive abilities, could be administered in about an hour, and reliably distinguished among "dull," "normal," and "bright" students as identified by the children's teachers (Terman, 1925).

What Terman Did

In 1916 Binet's work came to the attention of Lewis Terman, a professor at Stanford University. Terman translated and published a revised version of the Binet scale for use with American children. The test was called the Stanford-Binet (Terman, 1925). Terman's intelligence scale used a series of "age-graded tasks" designed to measure the average intellectual performance of subjects age 3 to 13. Terman gave his test to 1000 middle-class American children in California in order to establish performance norms against which an individual child could be compared. Thus, he established the first test that rendered a numerical measure of a person's performance on an intelligence test in relation to the performance of other examinees at the same age, which was called an _intelligence quotient:_ an _IQ._ Originally, the number was meant to signify a percentage of the child's actual age—a ten-year old with an IQ of 120 was thought to be in some way the intellectual equal of a twelve-year-old—but that meaning has long since been discarded.

According to the norms established for the Stanford-Binet, the interpretation of scores can be viewed in Table 1. A consistent feature of all modern IQ tests is the "normal distribution" of scores around an IQ of 100. That is, the patterning of scores made by test-takers in each age group is governed by a mathematical principle that produces a smooth curve (called a deviance curve) sloping in each direction from the middle of the population—the

Table 1

The Meaning of an IQ Score Obtained from the Stanford-Binet

An IQ of	Equals or exceeds % of the population
160	99.99
140	99.3
135	98
130	97
125	94
120	89
115	82
110	73
105	62
100	**50**
95	38
90	27
85	18
80	11
75	6
70	3
65	2
62	1

score at the center of all the scores. Whatever that number happens to be (it is not a numerical result of the test—it certainly has no relation to a 100% score) its value in arranging all the scores is assigned as 100. That score, then, as represented by 100, is made the center of the curve devised so as to give us a reasonably meaningful set of relationships among the scores on it. For rough purposes we can say that the test-taker whose score is now given a value of 120 is "20% smarter" than the one at 100.

According to the norms established for the Stanford-Binet, the interpretation of scores can be viewed in Table 1 in relation to percentile ranks. Percentile ranks are provided to communicate the percentage of age peers the test taker outperformed. For example, an 8-year-old girl, who scored at the 82nd percentile (i.e., an IQ score of 115), performed better than 82% of 8-year-olds. A man 22 years old who scored at the 11th percentile (i.e., an IQ score of 80), scored higher than 11% of his age peers.

Approximately a decade after the development of the Stanford-Binet IQ test, researchers (Terman, 1925; Hollingworth, 1942) began studying gifted children based on the standardized measure of intelligence quotients. Research by Terman and Hollingworth was conducted in order to clarify the definition of giftedness, to refute the existing stereotypes that intellectually or mentally gifted children would be physically frail and weak, and to examine contributions of the gifted adult.

Terman's (1925) now classic study began in 1921 with approximately a thousand children having measured intelligence quotients (IQ) of 140 and above according to the Stanford-Binet Intelligence Test (cited in Terman, 1925). By 1922, the group number for the study was 1,470 subjects; later, 58 siblings of the original number were added, bringing the total number of subjects to 1,528 (Terman & Oden, 1959).

Throughout Terman's study, he continued to examine and refine the use of standardized tests. In 1969, Terman concluded that measures of intelligence should correlate with school "educability" as represented by arithmetic reasoning, grasp of analogies, language completion, naming opposites, and interpreting passages. By 1975 he would describe giftedness as follows:

> Children of IQ 140 or higher are, in general, appreciably superior to unselected children in physique, health, and social adjustment: markedly superior in moral attitudes as measured either by character tests or by trait ratings: and vastly superior in their mastery of school subjects as shown by a three-hour battery of achievement tests. (Terman, 1975, p. 9)

Terman studied his subjects for 35 years, which resulted in the publication of five volumes, *The Genetic Studies of Genius* (Terman & Oden, 1959). Largely due to the contributions of Terman, programs for gifted children were developed in Los Angeles, Cleveland, and New York as early as 1920 (Witty, 1958). Terman's work thus became the basis for identifying giftedness in early programs, and standardized IQ tests such as the Stanford-Binet became the foundation for determining giftedness.

What Hollingworth did

Leta Stetter Hollingworth (1942) also studied giftedness by engaging in a longitudinal study, hers of twelve children with an IQ of 180 and above. Hollingworth, whose focus was on the psychological well-being of gifted individuals, focused on the contributions and impact of the gifted on society. She drew the following conclusions about giftedness in her book, *Children Above 180 IQ*:

> Turning to positive considerations, we know that these pupils, they and no others, will possess as adults those mental powers on which the learned professions depend for conservation and advancement. Also, we know that they will be the literary interpreters of the world of their generation. And they will be the ones who can think deeply and clearly about abstractions like the state, the government, and economics. We know this because we have seen a group like this "grow up" over a period of fifteen years, and we know what "became" of every one of them. (p. 36)

More Recent Assessments

Given the ingeniousness of the these assessment instruments and based on conclusions drawn by researchers about the valuable social contributions made by such highly intelligent persons, it might appear that IQ assessment instruments will be all that educators require to effectively identify giftedness. However, nothing could be farther from the truth. While early research established an invaluable knowledge base for educators concerning the assessment and identification of gifted individuals based on high IQ, it only began the quest for answers about giftedness.

Do intelligence measures and school achievement always indicate giftedness? Perhaps a closer examination of eminent adults such as Sir Isaac Newton, one of the towering intellects of all human history, who "was a failure throughout much of his school career and considered to be an idle tinkerer until he formulated the Laws of Gravity" (Smutny & Blocksom, 1990, p. 1) prompted educators to reevaluate the validity of IQ scores and academic achievement as the sole determinants of human intellectual potential or ability. Miller (1981) noted that hidden characteristics might exist in individuals with exceptional intellectual and creative potential:

> The list of universally recognized talented people whose gifts were *not* identified by the professionals in their youth is distressingly long. Winston Churchill, Thomas Edison, Albert Einstein, Emily Dickinson …to name but a few examples. (p. 6)

Another concern emerged in more recent times about the sole use of IQ tests to determine giftedness. In the golden days of research from the early to mid 1900's when IQ was the primary means of identifying the gifted, there was no representation from low socioeconomic, minority, or rural populations. Ironically, these same groups have the least representation in programs for gifted children to this day.

In the 1980s and 1990s, researchers (e.g., Clark, 1992; Feldman, 1982; Gardner, 1983; Sternberg, 1988) who examined the negative impact of using a single IQ score to determine giftedness expanded theories of intelligence. For example, Clark's 1988 definition of giftedness consisted of a combination of complex brain functions, which might manifest itself in cognitive or academic aptitude, creative behavior, leadership, or visual and performing arts. In agreement with Clark, Howard Gardner expanded the definition of giftedness by including more than an IQ score to determine intellectual ability. Based on his research, originally Gardner hypothesized about seven intelligences, comprising linguistic, logic, musical, spatial, bodily kinesthetic, interpersonal, and intrapersonal abilities. He has recently included naturalist and existential intelligence.

Gardner's concept of intelligence went beyond the cognitive processes measured on IQ tests, such as the Stanford-Binet used in Terman's study, and included the use of interactive activities to locate and nurture the seven intelligences. For example, research was conducted at Tufts University whereby children engaged in activities that focused on the seven original categories. The children with above average ability in one or a combination of the seven, according to trained teacher observation, were given further programming to foster and develop those strengths (Hatch & Gardner, 1988).

Another expansion to the theories of intelligence and conception of giftedness was that of Sternberg (1988). Like Gardner, Sternberg's triarchic theory supported that intelligence was more than cognitive processes and knowledge acquisition (i.e., recalling and applying acquired knowledge), which may be measured on intelligence tests. In the triarchic theory, intelligence includes contextual skills (the ability to adapt to the environment) and experiential skills (being able to transfer past problem solving to new situations).

In 1988, Sternberg explained intellectual giftedness in terms of the triarchic theory as follows:

> The triarchic theory of intellectual giftedness asserts that intelligence must be understood in terms of three aspects: (a) the internal world of the individual; (b) the external world of the individual; and (c) the interface between these two worlds as it unfolds through experience. Practical intelligence involves the ability to (a) select environments that are appropriate for one's talents, (b)

adapt to those environments, and (c) shape those environments in ways which enhance one's talents (p. 143).

Gardner and Sternberg were pioneers in the reformation of the 80s and 90s. But other noteworthy contributors to the expanded definition of intelligence and models defining giftedness are: Renzulli's three ring model of giftedness (1986); Gagne's differentiated model of giftedness/talents (1995); Tannenbaum's psychosocial model (1983). Each of these models defines giftedness in broad terms, using both creative potential and production as an important component toward recognizing intelligence.

During the first decade of the 21st century, researchers (Smutny, 2003; Ryser, 2004) have continued to explore appropriate measures for identifying giftedness and have added to the body of knowledge related to a broadened definition. Conclusions among these authors are the same—test scores often limit educators' perceptions of a child's ability. Especially when considering creative problem solving and reasoning or creative potential, all agree that intelligence quotients are not sufficient. A common recommendation for recognizing children's intellectual and creative potential is the use of behavior checklists, portfolios of student work, or interviews with the children who have been nominated for program services.

Putting Together the Old and New

The use of standardized test scores to determine giftedness has been labeled *traditional assessment* (Coleman & Gallagher, 1995; Nelson & McCann, 1989). For approximately half a century from the 1920s to the 1980s, traditional assessment was the predominant determinant of giftedness in schools. It has been only within the past thirty years that researchers and educators have questioned the use of IQ to determine intellect or the sole use of IQ to determine giftedness. With expanded definitions of intelligence, expanded definitions of giftedness emerged. Within the more current theories such as Gardner, a performance-based identification philosophy is apparent. A performance-based assessment for determining giftedness includes observation by trained specialists to recognize certain student actions as "above average" and/or the examination of students' products as exemplary or exceptional.

In 2003, Pfeiffer did a survey of 64 experts in the field of gifted education. He asked them about the three greatest identification, assessment, and/or definitional issues in gifted education. Interestingly, all of their responses emphasized the shift from traditional to a more performance-based view of giftedness. Thus, while gains have been made in the ability to use performance-based guidelines, the quantification of subjective measures remains slightly problematic. Table 2 shows some of the advantages and disad-

Table 2
Advantages and Disadvantages of IQ Tests

Advantages	Disadvantages
Scores predict academic performance.	Tests do not sample non-academic skills.
Can identify gifted underachievers and those with learning disabilities	Tests can under-identify creativity.
Provides a profile of children's developmental strengths and needs	Tests will disadvantage children who are not confident at taking tests and for whom too much might be read into results.
Avoids the biases inherent in purely subjective assessments	IQ tests introduce their own errors.
Testing is a quick, relatively inexpensive way to sample reliably a broad range of academic skills.	Can only inadequately sample evaluation and divergent thinking skills and the multi-dimensional nature of intelligence
More valid than any alternatives	Only valid with respect to intellectual giftedness
Allows comparison between children, thus allowing educational programs to target the most needful	Scores imply that one's ability is innate, stable and fixed—which can be a self-fulfilling prophecy.

vantages of using IQ tests to assess giftedness. Table 3 displays advantages and disadvantages of performance-based measures.

What Marland Did

In 1971, Sidney Marland presented to the US Congress a definition for giftedness that included a variety of kinds of gifts and talents. This definition had been agreed upon by a majority of persons serving on an advisory panel to the US Office of Education. Once Marland presented the definition to Congress, it became (and remains) the most widely accepted and used description for schools that have made educational provisions for advanced learners. The definition is:

> Gifted and talented children are those identified by professionally qualified persons who, by virtue of outstanding abilities, are capable of high performance. Those are

Table 3

Advantages and Disadvantages of Performance-Based Assessments

Advantages	Disadvantages
Sample of non-academic skills in the collection of portfolios	Lack of empirical data that predicts academic success
Can view samples of creative writing and production	The lack of quantitative evidence for an identification committee to determine placement
Eliminates test anxiety or bias	Indicates strengths in talent areas but not in abstract thinking abilities toward problem solving
Observation of students' abilities in areas such as visual art, performing art, vocational arts, etc.	The lack of numerical and graph data to share with parents and other educators
Eliminates the use of abstract thinking as the sole criterion and examines productivity	The inability to place information on a profile or data sheet which condenses evidence of giftedness

children who require differentiated educational programs and/or services beyond those normally provided
by the regular school program in order to realize their
contribution to self and society. The abilities, either
potential or demonstrated, to be included are *general
intellectual ability, specific academic aptitude, creative or productive thinking, leadership ability, ability in visual and performing arts,* and *psychomotor ability.* This definition
includes approximately 3 to 5 percent of the school population.

This definition is inclusive of multiple abilities. Noticeably, it
leaves the means and measures whereby educators determine
these areas of giftedness open to the discretion of school professionals. Yet, based on this definition, the opportunity is available
to use a combination of traditional assessment measures and
nontraditional assessment procedures to determine giftedness
and consequently serve the learning needs of students who
require a different curriculum. Marland's definition and a multiple criterion based assessment procedure will be emphasized
further in future chapters.

Chapter 2

Defining Assessment
of Giftedness

What Giftedness is Being Assessed?

By assessment I mean the process of purposefully evaluating abilities and capabilities; the purpose being to inform decisions we will make as to essential and appropriate services to be provided. When addressing assessment procedures appropriate for determining giftedness, educators must be ever mindful that the *assessment procedures should be consistent with the definition for giftedness, which in turn should match the services available for the gifted.* This author's motto is: *If we identify it, we serve it.*

So, let's begin at the beginning: the definition. In planning identification procedures, it is necessary to define giftedness. Upon this definition, the assessment procedures are based. The definition should be a functional one; it is commonly guided by state mandates, rules, regulations, guidelines, or laws. Many state definitions for giftedness are based on Sidney Marland's 1971 address to Congress, which led to the enactment of Public Law 91-230. Notice that according to Marland's definition (see chapter 1 in this book), the students so classified either demonstrate or are capable of high performance in intellectual ability, academic content, creative thinking, leadership, the arts, or physical ability. Professionals identify them, and they require services different from regular education provisions.

While each state has adapted a definition that is comparable to Marland's definition, understanding state guidelines is important to educators of gifted children. In 1993, Passow and Rudnitski did an extensive study analyzing state policies for identification and education for the gifted. They examined legislation, regulations, rules, recommendations, and guidelines provided for 49 of the 50 states. While they discovered wide variability in use of models for identifying and planning programs for gifted learners, their investigation revealed that all 50 states have formulated policies that support the education of gifted and talented students.

The results of their analysis led them to some conclusions:

1. All 50 states have some form of policy in support of education for the gifted and talented.
2. The presence or lack of specific legislative mandates determines the nature of the program.
3. Approximately one-fifth of the states include *gifted and talented* under federal legislation for *special education*.
4. Policies for identifying giftedness range from broad (nontraditional) measures to specific standards including detailed lists of instruments.
5. There is great variance in definitions, identification procedures, and program requirements.
6. A few states consider that gifted students have distinct needs for programming to address social and emotional issues, not only intellectual ones.

Coleman and Gallagher (1995) investigated state guidelines for gifted identification. They identified nine categories used across 49 states to assess and identify giftedness. These categories are: intelligence, academic ability, creativity, artistic, leadership, critical thinking, psychomotor, psychosocial, and understanding one's cultural heritage. Table 4 illustrates the numbers of states using each category to determine giftedness.

Table 4

State Policies Regarding Types of Giftedness Identified

Type of Giftedness	Number of States Using This Category
Exceptional Intelligence	48
Academic Ability	48
Exceptional Creativity	41
Exceptional Artistic Ability	35
Leadership Skills	30
Critical Thinking Ability	15
Exceptional Psychomotor Ability	12
Psychosocial	8
Understanding of One's Cultural Heritage	5

At the time of this study, the mid-1990s, 34 states had legislative mandates for the identification of giftedness, yet only 30 states mandated programs for gifted students. Funding that accompanied the mandates varied widely, and most states provided only partial funding, leaving individual school districts to financially support both the identification and the programming needs of the gifted. Further, while only 34 states mandated gifted education, 47 required that someone within each school district should be the coordinator or supervisor of education for gifted students.

In 2010, information from www.hoagiesgifted.org and www.davidsongifted.org indicated that only 32 states had legislative mandates for gifted education programs. It is interesting to note that five of those 32 states do not provide any funding for services. Just as interesting is the notion that six states make funds available to schools for gifted education identification and programming, but they are not state mandated to provide services. Twelve states have no mandate and no funds are allocated at the state level for the purpose of serving the learning needs of the gifted. Despite the lack of money or support from state legislation, all but six states offer some recognition or program options for children who are exceptional learners. While that may sound promising, the reality is that many schools only offer advanced courses at the high school level as a school-wide means of serving gifted children's learning needs. Table 5 depicts the states that provide legislative mandates, funding, and services.

Table 5

State Mandates, Funds, and Services for Gifted Education

		Total
Mandate and Provide Funds	AK, AR, AZ, CO, FL, GA, ID, IA, IN, KS, KY, LA, ME, MN, MS, MT, NC, NE, NM, OH, OK, SC, TN, TX, WA, WV	27
Mandate But No Funds are Provided	AL, MD, NJ, OR, PA	5
No Mandate But Funds are Available to Serve Gifted Children	CA, HI, NI, ND, NV, UT	6
No Mandate: No Funds	CT, DC, DE, IL, MA, MO, NH, NY, RI, SD, VM, WY	12
Identify Giftedness and/or Serve Giftedness in Some Capacity	AK, AL, AR, AZ, CA, CO, CT, DE, FL, GA, HI, IA, ID, IL, IN, KS, KY, LA, ME, MD, MI, MN, MS, MO, MT, NC, NE, Nj, NM, NY, NV, OH, OK, OR, PA, SC, TN, TX, UT, VT, VA, WA, WI, WV	44
No Identification or Services of Any Kind	MA, ND, NH, RI, SD, WY	6
TOTAL NUMBER OF STATES PROVIDING INDENTIFICATION THROUGH OBJECTIVE AND/OR SUBJECTIVE MEASURES AND PROVIDING SERVICES TO GIFTED CHILDREN AT SOME LEVEL		44

Why Identify Giftedness?

Why should schools identify students with exceptional learning abilities and provide services for them? Gifted, talented, and creative students have learning needs different from those of their age peers, just as do students who have difficulties learning. For students needing "special education," professionals in all strands of education search out curriculum that matches their learning needs and strive to implement the strategies that will enhance their learning skills, and to enhance the development of the whole child. Should it be different for advanced learners—for the abstract thinker, for the advanced creative thinker, for the art prodigy, for the musically talented, or for the gifted athlete?

Consider other reasons for identifying and serving gifted, talented, and creative students. Marland (1971) ended his definition with a profound statement regarding why we should recognize, assess, and serve giftedness: "in order to realize their contribution to self and society" (p. 38). The benefits that can accrue both to the gifted individual and to her/his society are well recognized. The accomplishments of the gifted are evident in the contributions of, for example, Rachel Carson, Jonas Salk, Thomas Jefferson, Mary Bethune, to name just a few. They all had a lasting impact on education, ethics, government, and life itself. Also reflect on the contributions made by Thomas Edison on our lives through his countless invention—the phonograph, electric lamp, mimeograph, electric locomotive, and countless other products that have made our modern lives comfortable and abundantly blessed.

Thus, educators should desire and be determined to identify such individuals. One eminent individual will devise a way to insure the longevity of social security benefits, discover a cure for cancer, or invent new ways to make future lives more comfortable.

When Should Giftedness be Identified?

There has been much discussion and debate about when we should assess students for giftedness. Piagetian theory

(Piaget, 1952) might lead some to believe that if the development of formal operations, abstract reasoning, and creative potential do not occur until the approximate age of 9 or 10, it isn't feasible to assess giftedness until that time. But most programs for gifted children, in fact, offer some form of enrichment for all children in grades K, 1, and 2. During that time, educators may document potential giftedness. These schools usually do not test children for giftedness, collect performance-based data, or offer any direct program services until children are in the 3rd or 4th grades (indeed, around age 9). Most educators and directors of programs for gifted children receive nominations or referrals from many sources, including teachers, parents, peers, and self beginning about grade 3. Thus, the crucial first question for the educator of the gifted becomes: When should I begin receiving nominations and collecting data for the identification and consequent placement of students into programs for the gifted?

When enrichment occurs in grades K-2, classroom teachers and the educator of the gifted may document which children seem to exhibit characteristics of giftedness (e.g., advanced vocabulary, problem-solving ability, creative thinking ability, early mastery of reading, leadership skills, etc.). Typically, the facilitator or teacher of gifted children will go into each classroom and provide a 30-minute enrichment activity on a weekly basis. The teacher of gifted children will deliver lessons that encourage and engage children in creative thinking and abstract reasoning. During the lesson, the classroom teacher may complete a checklist that contains characteristics indicative of giftedness. By observing and documenting potential, the educators do not make any decisions about placement until accumulated evidence exists regarding the potential giftedness of the child. The evidence is usually combined with intelligence and creativity testing by about grade 3. At that time, a decision is made about learning needs and placement of the child in a program for gifted children. This process allows the children to mature and develop and discourages "labeling" the children at an early age.

Based on research funded by Javits grants, behavioral checklists have been developed appropriate for very young children. Specifically, partners of the Early Assessment for Exceptional Potential (EAEP) project (Shaklee, Whitmore, Barton, Barbour, Ambrose, Viechnicki, 1989) produced the list shown in Table 6. While these behavioral characteristics or identifiers were intended for the identification of precocious youth from low socioeconomic environments, the list is comprehensive and might be considered for a variety of populations.

While observation and behavioral checklists are a beginning toward identifying giftedness, there are advantages to identifying and providing services for the highly capable child even earlier than grade 3. Piirto (1999) indicates there is a risk that academically talented young children may learn to underachieve very soon into their school career. The reasons for this are varied but include a desire to be like other children rather than standing out academically—the social and emotional inability to deal with being different—and the lack of early childhood programs for precocious youngsters, leaving potential and ability undernourished. Thus, a goal for providing services to gifted youngsters is to decrease the risks of underachievement.

Some questions should be considered in summary. Should school districts seek to identify giftedness in very young children? Should school districts provide an enrichment program as a way of observing and documenting potential giftedness? Should a school district use both traditional and nontraditional methods of identifying giftedness? (My answer to each of those questions is "yes.")

All children should receive enrichment programming. A checklist of behavioral characteristics should exist for each child in the early grades in order to document potential giftedness of any and all children. But we must not overlook those children who enter school exhibiting characteristics of giftedness (e.g., reading, advanced vocabulary, creative production, leadership, etc). These children qualify for nomination and data collection toward the completion of a case study. Placement can and should occur and services should begin as soon as a child is placed. See Table 7.

Table 6

Identifiers from the Early Assessment for Exceptional Potential

Exceptional learner	a. exceptional memory
	b. learns quickly and easily
	c. advanced understanding of area
Exceptional use of knowledge	a. exceptional use of knowledge
	b. advanced use of symbol systems
	c. demands a reason for unexplained events
	d. reasons well in problem solving – transfers prior knowledge to new situations
Exceptional generator of knowledge	a. highly creative behavior
	b. does not conform to typical ways of thinking
	c. enjoys self-expression of ideas, feelings, or beliefs
	d. keen sense of humor
	e. highly developed curiosity about causes, future, the unknown
Exceptional motivation	a. perfectionism
	b. shows initiative: self-directed
	c. high level of inquiry and reflection
	d. long attention span when motivated
	e. leadership: desire and ability to lead
	f. intense desire to know

Table 7

Enriching and Identifying Potential Giftedness

When	Who	What
Grades K, 1, 2	All	Enrichment Class
	All	Document Potential Giftedness
	Enters School Exhibiting Characteristics of Giftedness	Nominate/Refer; Collect Data for Case Study
Grades 3 & 4	Exhibits Characteristics of Giftedness	Nominate/Refer; Collect Data for Case Study
Grades 5 & 6	Exhibits Characteristics of Giftedness	Nominate/Refer; Collect Data for Case Study
Grades 7–12	Exhibits Characteristics of Giftedness	Nominate/Refer; Collect Data for Case Study

Chapter 3

Assessment Procedures and Instruments

Where Does the Process Begin?

We defined and explored measures, both traditional (the use of standardized tests) and nontraditional (based on performance such as creative production), for identifying giftedness. We established the need for identifying and serving students who are gifted, talented, and/or creative. Consequently, the answer to all questions about when identification of giftedness should begin was: at once (that is, upon the student's entering school).

In the educational world of Utopia, where unlimited money, time, and human resources are available, *all* students are assessed for giftedness. In Utopia, educational programs are established specific to each child's individual strengths, gifts, or talents. But, since we cannot get to Utopia from here, we must use a different procedure to begin the process of identification.

Using Marland's definition to guide the identification process, the procedure will be laid out as a series of steps. The first step is nomination, or as it is sometimes called, referral. After a student has been nominated or referred, a collection of data begins. This process includes tests, questionnaires, and/or behavior checklists. Tests may include tests of cognitive performance ability, achievement, and creativity. Task commitment, motivation, and leadership are usually measured by rating scales. A portfolio of products may also be collected in the process of data collection. Information from parents, teachers, and the individual, along with test scores and portfolio samples, are collected. Finally, all the information is collated into a case study.

Screening, Nomination, or Referral

In this text a distinction is made between screening and nomination. A *screening* procedure for our purpose is a process whereby an educator reviews existing data in order to determine the potential of students. In other words, standardized achievement tests given to all children within the school district might be screened by a classroom teacher, the educator of gifted students, or the counselor, to call attention to any child who scores at the 90th percentile or above in any academic area or on the total battery. Further, some school achievement tests render a school ability index, which may indicate abstract thinking or reasoning ability according to that measure. These scores might also be used in a screening procedure. The next step for the professional who conducts the screening of existing scores should be the nomination or referral of the child.

The *nomination* or *referral* form is something that each individual district must develop according to its particular needs—though many of its elements will be standard. The completion of a nomination or referral form, which provides the educator with pertinent background information about the child, is the beginning of the identification process. Any child who has standardized test scores screened and scored at the 90 percentile or above in one or more categories should be nominated or referred. Any child who scored at the 90 percentile or above on a school ability index should come under consideration for assessment. Any child who exhibits personality characteristics of giftedness (exceptional problem-solving or creative ability, advanced or rapid learning, etc.) should be nominated or referred for assessment. A sample is provided in Figure 1 of a nomination or referral form. For the purpose of illustration, a fictitious program name will be used in this text: TAG, Talented and Gifted.

The next step in the process is obtaining permission from parents to test the child. Again, testing will occur after the child has been nominated, based on the observation of characteristics of giftedness or by the screening of existing standardized tests that indicate potential giftedness. At this point, parents should receive a letter explaining the nomination process, the assessment procedures, and the program services. Figure 2 contains a sample letter for parents. Figure 3 contains an example of a permission-to-test form.

Once the nomination form is on file and permission to test has been secured, the collection of data may begin. We will consider a variety of assessment instruments available to the educator to assess cognitive reasoning.

Assessing Cognitive Abilities

In the following sections of this chapter, definitions associated with assessment may be useful to the reader. They can be previewed in Appendix A to assist with understanding any technical or functional terminology associated with concepts of assessment.

If the school or the district has resources available to hire or use a professional psychological examiner, testing for cognitive ability, abstract thinking, and/or verbal ability may be completed by such a person. The most widely used measures by certified examiners are the *Wechsler Intelligence Scale*—4th Ed. (WISC-IV) (Wechsler, 2003) for Children ages 6–16. A second test, the *Wechsler Preschool and Primary Scale of Intelligence—Revised (WPPSE-R)* (Wechsler, 2003) is designed for preschoolers between ages 4 and 6. The verbal subtests of Wechsler's tests are very similar to those

Figure 1
Sample Nomination Form

TAG: TALENTED AND GIFTED
NOMINATION FORM

Pleasant School District
1200 Pleasant Dr.
Goodville, TN 77880
(456) 789-1234

NOMINATION FOR: _____

who is in the _____ grade at _____School.

The teacher is _____.

Parents:_____

Address:_____

_____

Home phone _____

Phone Work:_____Work: _____

e-mail: _____ e-mail: _____

Name of Person Nominating: _____

Circle one: Parent,   Teacher,   Other School Person,   Self,   Peer,   Other

Please list characteristics you have observed which led you to make this nomination.

If there is documentation (creative writing samples, evidence of advanced academic performance, pictures of projects, etc.) indicating exceptional potential, please include copies with this nomination.

Send to: Jane Doe, TAG Coordinator at the address above or place in the TAG box at your school.

Figure 2
Sample Parent Letter

Pleasant School District
1200 Pleasant Dr.
Goodville, TN 77880
(456) 789-1234

Dear [Mr./Mrs/Ms.   ],

A nomination for the TAG (Talented and Gifted) Program has been received for your [daughter, Maria]. Programs for gifted children are mandated by the state department of education and are designed to help each child develop her or his potential to the fullest.

Students are placed in the program on the basis of exceptional cognitive, creative, or academic abilities and task commitment. Each child is considered carefully, using IQ tests, creativity assessments, standardized achievement test scores, rating scales, and portfolio samples. Following the compilation of scores, a committee reviews all the data. (No student's name is revealed to the committee.) If the majority of the scores and evidence fall within the excellent and superior range, the committee will recommend placement.

Once a child is placed, services are based on the child's learning needs. Students in grades K-2 receive a session of enriched instruction by the TAG teacher once a week. They also receive direct services. Students in grades 3 through 6 receive services through Think Tank, a special class they attend for 3 hours a week. A management plan also exists for each child receiving services. This plan is a cooperative effort between regular classroom teachers, the TAG teacher, the child's parents, and the child to provide a curriculum that is appropriate through all academic content or subjects.

Students in grades 7 through 12 are served through a management plan and independent study program. These students also have the opportunity to participate in advanced placement coursework, Quiz Bowl, Future Problem Solving, and Leadership Seminar.

In order for us to compile a clear academic picture of Maria, we need your permission to test her. Attached you will find a permission form. Please sign it and send it back to school, or mail it directly to our office. Testing, identification, and placement take approximately two months. We will also ask that you attend a conference following the placement decision by the committee to review Maria's case and to help plan her program. We will notify you when that point comes.

Thank you in advance for your cooperation. We look forward to meeting you. If you have any questions, don't hesitate to contact me at jdoe@gcs.edu or at (456) 123-6777.

Sincerely,
Jane Doe
TAG Coordinator

Figure 3
Sample Permission to Test Form

I give permission for my child _____

who is in _____ grade at _____

to be given a test of individual ability and creativity.

NO, I do not wish for my child_____

who is in _____ grade at _____

to be tested at this time.

_____
     Parent/Guardian Signature

_____
           Date

on the Stanford-Binet described in Chapter 1. These measure vocabulary, general knowledge, understanding of ideas and concepts, and arithmetic reasoning. Nonverbal skills are also measured through the ability to assemble puzzles, solve mazes, reproduce geometric designs with colored blocks, and rearrange sets of pictures to tell a story.

While the *WISC-IV* (Wechsler, 2003) and *Stanford-Binet, Fifth Edition* (Roid, 2003), are widely used by schools for the diagnosis of learning deficits, only certified examiners are permitted to administer them. However, most schools depend upon the facilitator/ teacher or coordinator/administrator of the program for gifted children to test for giftedness. And most facilitators of gifted programs are not psychological examiners. In such cases, there are instruments that can be given to measure cognitive task performance such as problem solving, abstract thinking, or intellectual reasoning. By using such measures, we are assessing these abilities compared to a group used to "norm" the assessment. We are also acting on the assumption that this score is indicative of just one form of giftedness: intellectual.

Some examples of other cognitive performance assessments that an educator (rather than a certified psychologist) can administer are: *Cognitive Abilities Test—Form 6* (Lohman & Hagen, 2000); *Differential Aptitude Test* (Bennett, 1982); *Henmon-Nelson Test of Mental Ability* (Nelson & French, 1973); *Kaufman Brief Intelligence Test 2* (Kaufman & Kaufman, 2004); *Matrix Analogies Test: Naglieri Nonverbal Ability Test Individual Administration* (Naglieri, 1996); *Otis-Lennon Mental Ability Test—7th Edition* (Otis & Lennon, 1995); *Slosson Intelligence Test* (Slosson, Nicholson, & Hibpshman, 1996); *SOI (Structure of the Intellect) Learning Abilities Test: Screen for Atypical Gifted* (Meeker & Meeker, 1975); *Woodcock-Johnson III Tests of Cognitive Abilities* (McGre & Mather, 2003). Let's consider and compare the potential use of each one of these measures through the use of a chart, which describes the cognitive skills tested, the age range of participants, the time required for testing, and the publishing information. Table 8 displays information about cognitive performance assessments.

A school must make a decision about the use of one, if any, test of cognitive ability by the school district. But when assessing potential giftedness, exceptional cognitive processing is only one realm in which giftedness might manifest itself. Another area for consideration when identifying gifted children is creativity.

Assessing Creativity

Following World War II, and especially in the 1950s and 1960s after Sputnik put the Russians ahead of the United States in space exploration, creative problem-solving became an emphasis for public schools. It was a time of flourishing industry and growth, and the United States wanted to be "first." In the 1950s, the University of Buffalo's Creative Education Foundation instituted a program for students that promoted creative problem solving

Table 8

Cognitive Performance Assessments Relevant to Giftedness

Assessment instrument	Skills assessed	Age group and time	Published by
Cognitive Abilities Test *	Reasoning and problem solving: verbal, quantitative, and nonverbal reasoning ability	Grades K–12	Riverside Publishing Company Lohman, D., and Hagen, E. (1993)
Differential Aptitude Test	Verbal reasoning, numerical ability, abstract reasoning, clerical speed and accuracy, mechanical reasoning, space relations, spelling, and language usage	Grades 7–12 Six subtests, 12–25 mins each	Harcourt Brace Educational Measurement Bennett, G. K. (1982)
Kaufman Brief Intelligence Test 2	Verbal and abstract thinking: Word recall, expressive vocabulary, pictorial analogies, matrix analogies	Ages 4–99 50–70 mins	American Guidance Service Kaufman, A. S., and Kaufman, N. L. (2004)
Matrix Analogies Test: superceded by *Naglieri Nonverbal Ability Test Individual Administration*	Nonverbal reasoning abilities with pictorial and figural analogies	Ages 5–17 30 mins	The Psychological Corporation (MAT - Expanded Form) Naglieri, J. A. (1985)
Otis-Lennon School/Mental *Ability Test* *	Numerical ability, abstract reasoning, space relations	Primary, Elem, Intermed, and Advanced 50 minutes	The Psychological Corporation Otis, A., & Lennon, R. (1967)
Slosson Intelligence Test	Verbal, performance and memory, analogies	Ages 4–adult 20–35 mins	Slosson Educational Publication, Inc. Slosson, R.; revised by Nicholson, C., and Hibpshman, T. (1996 – R)

*group administered assessment

Table 8 *(continued)*
Cognitive Performance Assessments Relevant to Giftedness

Assessment instrument	Skills assessed	Age group and time	Published by
SOI (Structure of the Intellect) Abilities Test: Screen for Atypical Gifted	A comprehensive assessment of "intellect"—(does not render IQ) comprehension, memory and problem solving	Primary to Adult 55 mins	SOI Systems Meeker, M., and Meeker, R. (1975)
Woodcock-Johnson III Tests of Cognitive Ability	Information-processing ability, working memory, planning, naming speed, and attention	Ages 2–90 60 mins	Riverside Publishing: Houghton Mifflin Woodcock, R., McGre, K., and Mather, N. (2003 – R)

(Osborn, 1963). This was called the Parnes-Osborn Model. In this model, students used a systematic format for reaching a conclusion to a problem: Data Finding, Problem Finding, Idea Finding, Select a Solution, and Acceptance Finding. By following these steps, students clarified a problem by collecting information, stating the problem, generating solutions to the problem, making decisions about the problem and solutions, and implementing the solution.

From this early work came an abundance of research and models (Feldhusen & Clinkenbeard, 1986; Treffinger, 1987; Torrance, 1987) that emphasized creativity. Thus, creativity was incorporated into the assessment of, and educational programs for, gifted children. Treffinger (1987) gave seven reasons creativity should be considered valuable to the education of children. They were: (1) to focus on the strengths of individual students, (2) to recognize that IQ and achievement testing are limited, (3) to help schools, which must be practical, compare themselves to standardized norms, (4) to expand the basic profile of students in the realm of creativity, (5) to help teachers find and use their own creativity, (6), to contribute to research about nurturing creative behaviors, and (7) to implement creativity as something that can be understood rather than something mysterious. Further, Piirto (1999) gave reasons why creativity became an integral part of education for the gifted and talented. Among those reasons were: (1) to increase students' numbers of creative products, (2) to increase students' quality of creative products, (3) to identify children with academic, visual art, and performing art talents, and (4) our nation still wants creative people who can compete internationally.

In this section we will examine two of the most highly used tests of creativity, which render scores in various realms of divergent thinking. These tests are *Torrance Tests of Creative Thinking* (Torrance, 2008) *Williams Creativity Assessment Packet (CAP)* (Williams, 1993) Another assessment for giftedness which includes creativity will also be described: SAGES—*Screening Assessment for Gifted Elementary Students* (Johnsen & Corn, 1992)..

All the above are assessment instruments administered to students. Each one quantifies creativity from standard scores to percentile scores. There is a variety of creativity checklists, questionnaires, or rating scales. Of those, the author of this text will provide information regarding *Scales for Rating the Behavioral Characteristics of Superior Students* (Renzulli, Smith, White, Callahan, Hartman, & Westberg, 2002) and the *Gifted and Talented Evaluation Scales* (Gilliam, Carpenter, & Christensen, 1996)

The *Torrance Test of Creative Thinking (TTCT)* by E. Paul Torrance has publications dates ranging from 1966 through 2008. The TTCT will assess creative thinking abilities of students in fourth grade through adulthood. The cost of one administrator set (with 20 test booklets) is approximately $41.00. The examiner's kit is approximately $30.00. There is a form A and B for figural and verbal creativity abilities. The publisher is Scholastic Testing Service, Inc., 480 Meyer Rd., Bensenville, IL 60106; telephone number, 800-642-6787. The website is www.ststesting.com. The assessment renders scores for fluent, flexible, original, and elaborate thinking. The *Torrance Tests of Creative Thinking* are accompanied by separate norms and technical manuals for both the verbal and figural forms.

Separate scoring guides for each form, a separate 44-page review of research on the TTCT, and three additional monographs are included.

The separate publication reviews many studies of the TTCT's validity, by a variety of researchers. It includes extensive documentation of content, concurrent, and construct validity, including several short-term and long-term predictive validity studies. Interscorer reliabilities are reported in excess of .90 from numerous studies. Test-retest reliabilities and alternate-form reliabilities are presented from many published reports with the results ranging from .59 to .97. The tests are easy to administer, and may be administered to groups from grades 4 and above. The figural form requires 30 minutes of working time, and the verbal form requires 40 minutes of working time. The directions for administration are presented clearly and in detail. There are detailed scoring instructions. However, scoring may take 20 minutes per student and requires careful study of the manual. The publisher offers a scoring service. The cost is approximately $6.00 per student and requires about 6 weeks for the return of the results.

The advantages of the TTCT are strong reliability, recognition of creative potential, and form A and B to use as pre- and posttests. The disadvantages are tediousness, time needed for scoring, and the lack of predictive validity.

The *Williams Creative Thinking Assessment Packet* was developed by Frank Williams in 1980. It tests children ages 6–18. The kit costs approximately $109.00 and consists of tests of divergent thinking and divergent feeling, and a parent/teacher rating scale. It is published by Pro-Ed Inc., 8700 Shoal Creek Boulevard, Austin, TX 78757: phone 800-897-3202. The website for ordering is: www.proedinc.com. The divergent thinking test portion is a three-page assessment with four boxes on each page. Each box contains lines and shapes. The test taker is to begin with the lines and shapes given and construct unique pictures— to incorporate the lines and shapes into new pictures. A score is obtained for fluency, flexibility, originality, and elaboration. The divergent feeling test is a 50-item questionnaire for the student to complete; it assesses curiosity, imagination, complexity, and risk-taking. The Parent Rating Scale is also a 50-item questionnaire, which parents answer on a Likert scale of *always, sometimes,* or *seldom.* The validity and reliability data are stated, but no specific descriptions are provided of the samples whereby data was obtained. A scoring guide for the Test of Divergent Thinking is used to assist with the interpretation of scores (see Appendix B).

The advantages of using the Williams CAP are the form A and B for pre- and post-assessment, an easy guide and specific examples for scoring, and the availability of parent feedback through a rating scale. The disadvantages are the lack of reliability and validity data, and the link made between elaboration and asymmetry is questionable.

Last, the *Screening Assessment for Gifted Elementary Students* (Johnsen & Corn, 1992) is administered to students in kindergarten through 3rd grade. It requires about 30 minutes. The price is $280.00 for the complete kit. It can be ordered from Pro-Ed Inc. Its subtests sample aspects of two of the most commonly used areas for identifying young gifted students' aptitude and achievement. Aptitude is measured by the reasoning subtest. The child is asked to solve analogical problems by identifying relationships among pictures and figures. General information assesses achievement. The child answers questions about everyday concepts and those introduced in the primary school years by selecting from a series of pictures, symbols, or words.

All of the SAGES subtests may be administered in small groups or individually. Standard scores and percentile ranks are provided for subtests, and full-scale scores are given for both gifted and regular samples. The test was standardized on a large, nationally representative sample of more than 2,500 regular students and 1,000 gifted students. Data are provided supporting test-retest and internal consistency reliability and content, construct, and criterion related validity. Validity studies indicate that the SAGES scores differentiated among groups with the gifted sample. A strength of the SAGES is the comprehensive package including cognitive, academic, and creative talents. A drawback to using this measure for creativity is it only assesses divergent production.

Finally, the GATES (Gifted and Talented Evaluation Scales) is a questionnaire completed by parents or teachers. It contains five sections of 10 questions regarding the creative behaviors of a child. These include intellectual, academic, creativity, leadership, and art abilities. Table 9 shows a comparison of creativity assessments.

Assessing Task Commitment, Motivation, and Leadership

To recapitulate the assessment procedure to this point: the process begins with the nomination of a student for assessment. The nomination may be made by the parent (who knows the child better than anyone), teacher, self, peers, or anyone who observes characteristics of giftedness. The definition used by the school district, which is typically guided by the state department of education, will dictate what kind of assessment procedure is in place. In other words, if the state definition for giftedness includes exceptional cognitive, creative, academic, and leadership abilities, then it is those kinds of assessment measures that should be used in the identification process.

We have examined a variety of assessment instruments that measure cognitive abilities such as analogies, problem solving, abstract thinking, sequential reasoning, etc. A variety of creativity assessments have been described. Next, we will consider how to assess task commitment, motivation, and leadership.

Earlier in this chapter, the *Scales for Rating the Behavioral Characteristics of Superior Students* by Renzulli, Smith, White, Callahan, Hartman, and Westberg (2002) was mentioned. The scales are completed by teachers or parents and include learning, creativity, motivation, leadership, artistic, musical, dramatics, communication (precision), communication (expressiveness), and planning characteristics. Each scale contains approximately

Table 9
Comparison of Creativity Assessments

Assessment Instrument	Skills assessed	Age Group and time	Published by
Torrance Test of Creative Thinking (TTCT)	Fluency, flexibility, originality, elaboration	K–adult 30 mins	Scholastic Testing Service, Inc. Torrance, E. P. (2008–R)
Williams Creativity Assessment Packet (CAP)	Fluency, flexibility, originality, elaboration, curiosity, complexity imagination, risk-taking	Age 6-18 Divergent Thinking 20–30 mins Divergent Feeling 20 mins	Pro-Ed Inc. Williams, F. (1993)
SAGES– Screening Assessment for Gifted Elementary Students	Divergent production	K–3 55 mins	Pro-Ed Inc. Johnsen, S., and Corn, A. (1992)

Checklists	Skills assessed	Time and who completes	Published by
Renzulli-Hartman Creativity Scale in the Scales for Rating Behavioral Characteristics of Superior Students	Imagination, sense of humor, originality, risk-taking, elaboration	10 mins Teachers or Parents	Creative Learning Press Renzulli, J. S. (2002–R)
Gifted & Talented Evaluation Scales	Subtests include creativity	5–10 mins per scale Teachers or Parents	Pro-Ed Inc. Gilliam, J.E., Carpenter, B. D., & Christensen, J. R. (1996)

10 to 15 items. The items are rated on a scale of never (1), very rarely (2), rarely (3), occasionally (4), frequently (5), always (6). A score is calculated by adding the column total, multiplied by the weight (1–6) of the Likert scale. The total for each column is added to render a scale total or raw score. A guide and formula is provided to calculate local percentile rank norms.

While there are few scales that predict motivation and task commitment other than the Renzulli, et al. Scales, there are multiple sources and forms of leadership scales. For example, *Leader Behavior Questionnaire*, (Sashkin, 2001), *Leadership Q-Sort Test* (Cassell, 1965), and *Leadership Opinion Questionnaire* (Edwin, 1978) are just a few. However, the majority of the existing leadership questionnaires or scales are more applicable to business leaders than they are to students.

One scale, *The Leadership Skills Inventory* (LSI) (Karnes & Chauvin, 2000) was devised for use with school-age children. This scale is used with students from grades 4 to 12. The LSI identifies areas of strength and weakness in leadership and can be readministered to measure growth and improvement over time. It also measures nine relevant dimensions of leadership: fundamentals of leadership, written communication skills, speech communication skills, character-building skills, decision-making skills, group dynamic skills, problem-solving skills, personal skills, and planning skills. The scale is rated by the participant according to *almost always* (3), *on many occasions* (2), *once in a while* (1), or *almost never* (0). The points are tallied for each scale. A T-Score chart is available for interpreting raw scores.

Interpreting Scores

While this text is not intended to be a technical manual for statistical analysis, it is important that any facilitator of gifted children be able to administer, score, and transfer scores into usable and understandable terms. Later, in Chapter 7, a profile sheet will be presented illustrating the use of multiple measures and the use of a chart to make the data easy to understand.

Each standardized test manual will have a set of directions for administering the assessment. For example, it will contain information about the appropriate age or grade level, the amount of time given to students at various levels. Typically, a scoring guide will give step-by-step instructions for scoring and interpreting scores. Almost all assessment instruments have a chart depicting the transfer of standard or raw scores (typically, the number of correct responses) to a percentile rank, the standard deviation above and below the mean, and/or stanine. Many assessments will use descriptive categories. For example, if a student's standard score is 131, which is at the 98th percentile, the manual may also provide terms like *upper extreme* to accompany the number interpretations.

Refer to Appendix B, which contains a sample of a step-by-step guide for scoring and interpreting scores on the Williams Creative Assessment Packet (Williams, 1993). This illustration also includes the matrix used to chart scores for both components of the assessment.

While all the measures described herein are available for use by teachers, the observations by classroom teachers, facilitators of gifted children, counselors, or parent can be the most useful in identifying special talents. This is especially true when the teacher is in close communication with parents. With the use of a combination of assessment measures, observation, and collection of student products the identification procedures will be more accurate and effective.

Chapter 4

Identifying Giftedness Among Subpopulations

Masked Giftedness

Could it be that despite modern communication, transportation, and technology there remain "hidden" communities with idiosyncratic value systems that impact educational opportunities for gifted children? Are gifted children from northern corn fields, western deserts, southern cotton fields, or inner city streets being overlooked for program services when schools identify giftedness? We can be sure these communities exist, but perhaps certain conditions mask giftedness. To broaden our understanding of these issues, let us examine various components of each scenario.

Understanding Giftedness in the Rural Community

Some time ago, Spicker, Southern, & Davis (1987) examined some problematic issues related to rural communities and the identification of giftedness. Their research focused on small communities—

those with a population of 2,500 or less—because those were the ones defined as "rural" by government agencies that collect census data. They considered that in a school district with just 500 children, it might be calculated that 30 to 50 students would represent the gifted population. Divided by 13 grades, the number per grade becomes very small. If those children are subcategorized by intellectual ability, academic achievement, creativity, and leadership, financial justification for program establishment might be hard to establish (Spicker, et al., 1987).

However, in order to understand implications for identification and the needs of gifted children in rural environments, it is necessary to look beyond population size and consider the characteristics of people who reside in sparsely populated areas. It is equally important to examine conditions in which individuals from rural communities live. Historically, of all impoverished populations in the United States, 40 percent have occurred in rural settings; of the 250 poorest counties in the United States, 237 were in rural areas of the south (Spicker, et al., 1987).

Moreover, poor rural regions often maintain strong traditional cultural values that compete with academics, are less likely to have resources necessary for advanced academic programs, and have less spending per student because of their lower per capita income than that in metropolitan areas (Cross & Dixon, 1998; Lewis, 2000). In much of the early research (Bull, 1988; Gear, 1984; Howley, Pendarvis, & Howley, 1988; Spicker, et. al., 1987), professional literature focused on problems associated with the rural communities as they relate to the educational provisions for gifted children:

1. The lack of parental support for gifted programs due to a resistance to change. Parents in rural communities are less likely to initiate the establishment of gifted programs than parents in a large community.
2. Smaller faculties may mean fewer specialty teachers who are able to teach advanced courses. Thus, gifted children may miss out on current content.

3. Because support for such programs must come mainly from within the community, a rural school is more likely to be independent than to be able to seek help from outside sources when considering the needs of gifted children (for example, there may be no university nearby).

Nevertheless, many other characteristics can make rural settings a healthy environment for recognizing and serving giftedness. Some of the characteristics considered to be deterrent may be, in fact, advantageous. For example, small schools make individuation easier—teachers know their students individually—and cross-grade grouping for students who excel in any particular academic content is convenient (Cross & Stewart, 1998; Howley, 1994; Lewis, 2000). Other more positive characteristics relate primarily to the classroom teacher and the teacher of gifted children as they work closely together to recognize gifted abilities (Abell & Lennex, 1999; Plucker & McIntire, 1996).

We should pause here to say that, while some characteristics may apply generally, great diversity exists both among and within rural communities (Howley, 1994). There may be as much difference between rural children's backgrounds (e.g., isolated versus culturally mainstreamed and low income versus average or high income) as there is between rural and urban children. Based upon such an assumption, identification and program services may be as unique as the culture of the setting.

Understanding Giftedness Among Minority Populations

Identification among minorities should be another urgent priority for educators of gifted children. Numerous articles have been written (Davidson, 1992; Frasier, 1991; Valencia, 1985) about the lack of representation from African American, Hispanic, or American Indian populations in programs for the gifted. Many times the failure to provide for these bright children leads to frustration for all stakeholders.

The problems minority children encounter are sometimes related to discrimination. And while some might doubt that discrimination is still a factor today, the lack of recognition of giftedness among minorities is often recorded. Many times the need to recognize giftedness in minority groups is illustrated by gifted adults who went unrecognized as gifted students. Consider the words of South (1971):

> Why is it that such people as Doctors Daniel Hale Williams, first to perform open-heart surgery, and Charles Drew, the discoverer of the secret of preserving blood plasma, both blacks, remained unknown until their adulthood, when their genius could no longer be ignored, but screamed for recognition? The answer is simple: their race. It has remained a relatively hidden fact that the non-Caucasian populations of the world have borne some of its greatest geniuses. This can be demonstrated from history, a history that reveals the fact that nonwhite people of Asia, Africa, South America, and the Mediterranean countries have given to the world an immeasurable wealth of knowledge. (p. 33)

Additionally, language is essential to thought and reasoning in conjunction with effective communication. Limited language development may be an inhibitor to test-taking skills for minority students—especially, though not only, when English is a second language.

Understanding Giftedness Among the Economically and Experientially Disadvantaged

Many of the same issues that might impede the identification of gifted among rural settings also apply to children from urban settings. Many of the issues that impact poor test scores among the urban or rural children also impact minority students. At this point, we need to look for common factors among all these groups and find ways to nurture gifted potential and identify gifted intellectual and creative abilities among these populations. And the common denominator is low socioeconomic status and limited experiential backgrounds. The impeding factor to identifying gifted among rural, urban, and/or minority students is actually not skin color, it is economic or experiential deficits. Thus, we must find alternative ways to overcome the negative impact of this key element on identification of giftedness.

Identification of Gifted Among Subpopulations

We have established that any identification effort that concentrates on a single ethnic population becomes partial and selective. And that attention should be given to all disadvantaged children with poverty and environmental limitations. Following are some considerations for improving identification among those children.

There is consistency in the literature (e.g., Gear, 1984; Howley, 1994; Richert, 1987; VanTassel-Baska, 2002) concerning the inclusion of multi-criterion approaches for identifying gifted children from disadvantaged backgrounds. Howley (1994) has recommended using traditional standardized instruments but reestablishing norms or ranks to the local school population. This procedure consists of determining the mean for the school based on percentile rank, then administering a group IQ test to the students who score above the school mean. Students scoring in the top 25% of the group IQ test will represent 12.5% of the school population.

Gear (1984) recommended broadening the concept of assessment by placing emphasis on students' special abilities, interests, and needs rather than using IQ tests. The suggestion to broaden the concept of assessment is congruent with the philosophical reason for having a program to serve gifted children (i.e., to develop the potential of the children to be leaders within the community).

In one recent study (VanTassel-Baska, 2002), identification of economically disadvantaged and minority students for gifted programs was the focus. Performance assessment tasks were developed and used with more than 4,000 students in primary and intermediate grades. These performance assessment tasks resulted in finding an additional group of students who were African American and low-income children. The students represented those who would not have qualified for gifted programs using traditional measures.

In addition to using multiple means of identifying potential, tests that identify gifted students from culturally different backgrounds have been designed and may be considered appropriate to test potential giftedness. Richert (1987) recommended several culturally fair tests. *Cattel Culture-Fair Intelligence Series* (Cattel & Cattel, 1965), which can be administered in twenty-five minutes, was designed to eliminate environmental influences. The *Raven's Progressive Matrices* (Raven & Court, 1995) is untimed and tests abstract thinking. *Naglieri Nonverbal Ability Test Individual Administration* (Naglieri, 1996) and *The Cartoon Conservation Scales* (Deal & Yan, 1985), which is for elementary children only, may be given in a variety of languages. There are also tests geared toward non-English speaking students, which have been written in Spanish, French, or German, such as the *Group Inventory for Finding Creative Talent* (Aschbacher & Winters, 1992).

Some of the most recent and highly used assessment instruments for diverse populations are noted in Table 10.

Other Suggestions for Broadening Representation

There are suggestions in the literature for reducing bias and increasing the likelihood of accurate identification of giftedness among subpopulations. Suggestions are specific to minority (Ford, 1994), rural (Lewis, 2000), and economically disadvantaged (Richert, 1987), but they all have a common basis—making

Table 10
Assessment Instruments Used to Identify Giftedness Among Diverse Populations

Assessment Instrument	Skills assessed	Age Group and time	Published by
Matrix Analogies Test: superceded by *Naglieri Nonverbal Ability Test Individual Administration.*	Nonverbal reasoning abilities with pictorial and figural analogies	Ages 5–17 30 minutes	The Psychological Corporation (MAT–Expanded Form) Naglieri, J. A. (1996)
Raven's Progressive Matrices	Nonverbal assessment of perception and thinking ability	Ages 6–12 Untimed	Oxford Psychologists Press Raven, J. C., and Court, J. H. (1995 – R)
Universal Nonverbal Test of Intelligence	Memory and analytical reasoning	K-12 50 minutes	Riverside Publishing Bracken, B. A., & McCallum, R. R. (1997)

accommodations to assure the inclusion of all children in programs for the gifted. Some suggestions include:

1. There is no one-size-fits-all intelligence or achievement test. Multi-criterion-based procedures offer the greatest promise (Ford, 1994).
2. To be valid and reliable, assessment instruments must be culturally sensitive (Ford, 1994).
3. Teacher training is a key factor in nurturing potential and identifying giftedness among diverse groups.
4. Understanding parents and parent involvement are crucial.

Performance-based assessment procedures provide another way of focusing on exceptional potential and abilities without the bias of standardized or objective measures. The most frequently used means of performance-based measures is the use of portfolios. In the portfolio process, a collection of a student's work is made. Exemplary samples of creative writing or creative production are accumulated. Creative production may be captured through the use of photographs of student products. These samples may be presented to an identification committee the same as test scores or other objective measures. Samples of student project work or portfolio entries are typically judged by a rubric. See Appendix C for examples of portfolio entry rubrics.

While there is no single solution to the problem, changes in educational policy and the practice that support multi-criterion methods of identifying gifted students may help school systems more effectively locate gifted children. And, as classroom teachers and parents are educated and involved in the identification process, potential of the gifted children will be developed.

Giftedness does exist among rural, minority, and low socioeconomic populations. As definitions of giftedness are broadened, identification procedures and provision of services may also be transformed. Traditional methods of identifying giftedness will identify many of the gifted from diverse populations. However, when negative characteristics of the environment mask giftedness according to standardized measures, the use of multiple-criterion, re-normed standardized measures, culturally fair instruments, or performance-based measures are appropriate traditional means of locating giftedness.

Chapter 5

Discovering Potential in the Primary Grades

Distinguishing Exceptional Characteristics of the Gifted in Preschool and Primary Grades

Why do facilitators of programs for the gifted go into classrooms and provide enrichment activities for *all* children, especially in the primary grades? Some might answer the question in a variety of humorous ways, including (a) to give the classroom teacher a break, (b) to give the teacher of the gifted something to do, or (c) to satisfy the principal. While educators of the gifted know that nothing could be farther from the truth, there are many who do not understand why enrichment is often an integral part of the assessment process for identifying giftedness in young children. There are some important ways enrichment can greatly enhance the accurate identification of students who need a different curriculum—to nurture creative and critical thinking, to observe students' exhibition of exceptional or unique creative processes, and to document the curious and creative production of young children.

I am often asked, "Aren't all children curious and creative?" The answer is, yes. The next time you have the opportunity to listen to young children (ages 4–7) at play, notice their world of pretend. Their imaginary adventures range from journeys around the moon to slaying purple dragons. See their curiosity—they can't wait for you to turn the next page of the book, see what's around the next corner, or see what surprise is in the bag.

So, how can educators use creativity, including curiosity, as a measure for determining giftedness among primary students? First, we must define creativity and examine assessment according to this definition. In Chapter 3, creative assessment instruments were introduced. This chapter will extend the content therein.

Torrance (1962, 1977, 1987) may be the most influential of all researchers or authors on the subject of identifying and nurturing creative giftedness. Torrance's 1977 definition of creativity encompassed the process of sensing problems, forming ideas, modifying ideas, and communicating uniqueness within ideas. The original work by Torrance (Torrance, 1962) led to the development of an assessment instrument (i.e., *Torrance Test of Creative Thinking—Figural & Verbal: TTCT*), which was renormed in 2008. This instrument assesses and calculates scores for fluency (the number of ideas), originality (uniqueness of ideas), abstractness of titles (a measure of the ability to synthesize the idea expressed in the drawing), elaboration (amount of detail), and resistance to premature closure (the ability to keep the transformation open). The first sub-test of the figural test for creative thinking includes a colored egg shape in the center of the page which is used as the basis for an imaginative drawing. The third figural activity includes two pages of circles or parallel lines which again are incorporated into complete, meaningful, and clever drawings. The fluency score is simply a count of ideas listed or drawings made. Originality scores are based upon statistical infrequency norms. That is, each idea is listed in a table in the scoring guide, including examples for awarding 0, 1, or 2 points, depending upon how infrequently or rarely that idea is drawn by the group used to norm the test. Counting the number of details beyond the basic picture renders a score for elaboration. These details are things added to the basic shape or picture. If the test is hand scored, this author recommends that the same person score the assessment, thus ensuring some measure of consistency in the interpretation of details. A better alternative might be to send it to the testing company for scoring, at a slight expense.)

Torrance (1977) also made suggestions for teachers to include "creative ways of teaching." He suggested that teachers provide opportunities for creative behavior which include: (a) creating assignments that call for original work, (b) asking questions that call for productive thinking, (c) using materials that allow for a flow of thoughts, and (d) developing skills in the use of analogy. Another measure of creativity much used over the past two decades is the *Williams Creativity Assessment Packet* (1993). This packet contains three assessments: (a) a test of divergent thinking administered to the student, (b) a scale of divergent feeling answered by the test taker, and (c) a rating scale for parents or teachers. The divergent thinking assessment consists of 12 boxes; each box contains lines or shapes. The test-taker makes pictures using the lines and shapes, much like the *Torrance Test of Creative Thinking* (1998) and then titles each picture. The assessment is scored using fluency, flexibility, originality, and elaboration as the guidelines. The Divergent Feeling Inventory is a 50-item rating scale. It contains questions pertaining to curiosity, imagination, complexity, and risk taking. The Williams Scale is a 48-item rating scale of items used by parents or teachers to evaluate student creativeness.

An understanding of fluency, flexibility, originality, and elaboration as measures of divergent thinking or creative thinking is essential. Further, an understanding that these abilities can be measured using standardized assessment tools is important to the development of appropriate curriculum for enrichment.

Presenting Curriculum that Emphasizes Creativity

Now, back to the children and creative abilities. When presenting lessons based on enhancing potential, enriching the existing curriculum, and searching for giftedness, remember:

1. Presenting a systematic curriculum based on creative processes will enhance potential.
2. Basic skills from the regular classroom can be used and incorporated into curriculum developed to enrich creative thinking.
3. The observation skills of the facilitator of gifted children and the classroom teacher can and should be used to document giftedness among primary students.

The following is a specific lesson based on a model introduced in this text. It is the CREATE Model (Figure 4). This is a combination of all the many existing notions about teaching creative thinking and processes.

The practical application includes a sample lesson plan. This lesson contains three steps. First, in the *warm-up* stage, students will brainstorm ideas (fluency). Next, any answers that change categories (flexibility) will be noted. For example, students are brainstorming things that are green. As students share ideas, commonly they think "on a track." Some sample answers might be green beans, lettuce, green grapes, peas, a lime, etc. Of course, they are piggy-backing ideas about green food, so no flexibility has been demonstrated. The child who answers "alien" should be noted for "changing tracks." During a brainstorming, warm-up session, *originality* may also be expressed. When students are brainstorming "green things," the child who says "green with envy or jealousy" would be noted for original thought.

Following the warm-up phase, students will *interact* with a story. During this stage, they will analyze, make predictions, create new characters, and create new endings. Finally, students will be given a shape or line. They will create a picture using and including the line or shape in their picture (see Appendix D). This final stage is *creative production*. At this stage students will *elaborate* by adding details to the picture or giving the picture a title.

Through this systematic plan, the children will exercise (and thus enhance) their creative capabilities. Practicing a series of

Figure 4
The CREATE Model

CREATIVE PROCESS
      These lessons will emphasize fluency, flexibility,
      originality, & elaboration.

REACT & INTERACT
      During the lessons students will interact and react to
      one another's creative production.

ENHANCE KNOWLEDGE
      These lessons will enhance and enrich the classroom
      content.

ASSOCIATIVE PROPERTIES
      Students will associate and link basic skills and
      thinking skills.

THINKING SKILLS
      These lessons will utilize creative and analytical
      skills.

EVALUATE STUDENTS' PROGRESS
      Following each lesson, the students' creative products
      will be evaluated.

skills (academic, creative, analytical) will enrich the classroom content. Creative production will be demonstrated by students. Ultimately, gifted potential will be documented. The documentation will occur for students who have the most ideas during the use of fluency—those who think of an idea which is in a category all its own. For example, when brainstorming things about blue, the student who says "sad" would be documented. The child or children who create something very unlike the other children would receive a point for originality and the child who labeled her/his picture with something other than its literal object would receive a point for elaboration. For example, the child who draws a picture of a kitten, but instead of calling the picture "kitten," titles it, "Give me some milk." That child would receive a point for elaboration.

Educators of Enrichment

The purpose of enrichment-based curriculum, which emphasizes creative and critical thinking, is to document potential giftedness of primary students. This process works best in a cooperative setting, between the classroom teacher and the teacher of gifted students. For the most effective results, the teacher of gifted students presents a lesson to engage students in creative process and production. While students are processing and responding to the lesson, the classroom teacher documents the student's responses and reactions. This process is one form of assessment of giftedness.

The procedure was established by Kingore (1990), who devised one of the first observational checklists to include categories such as advanced language, analytical thinking, meaning-motivated, perspective, sense of humor, sensitivity, and accelerated learning. The original work by Kingore involved a checklist with students' names and listed behaviors that were indicative of characteristics of giftedness. The process involved the documentation of these characteristics during the presentation of a lesson. Kingore (2001) recently developed a more sophisticated guide for interpreting results and developed a parent assessment to accompany the observation and documentation of gifted attributes in young children. This author has used a simplified version by developing a chart that documents only the creative process and performance. See the sample documentation chart in Figure 5.

Figure 5
Documentation Chart for Exceptional Creativity

Creative Thinkers	Fluency (No. of Ideas)	Flexibility (Divergent Category)	Originality (Creativity Award)	Elaboration (Descriptive Title)	Comments
Adams, Brandon					
Brannon, Samuel					
Brahms, Toya					
Crafton, Ashley					
Curtis, Joshua					
Delaney, John					
Ellis, Jill					
Haynes, Michael					
Hancock, Issac					
Inman, Steven					
Johnson, Dawn					
Moore, Robert					
Perkins, Shelly					
Raymond, Jayce					
Sullivan, Angie					
Wallis, Tony					

An example of a lesson presented by the C.R.E.A.T.E. Model in order to document creative potential follows:

Figure 6
Sample Lesson According to CREATE

UNIT – IT'S ALL ABOUT BEARS!

Lesson 1 - Wishing on a Star
Objective: Students will use (CREATE) creative process while using various skills—listening, making predictions, and creating original products.

Before every lesson have children stand and follow this chant with movement accompanying.

Teacher says: Raise your right hand and tap, tap, tap, tap, tap on your "noggin"; raise your left hand and tap, tap, tap, tap, tap on your noggin. With both pointer fingers, we will tap, tap, tap, tap, tap on our noggin. Now, move your head around and round. Move your shoulders up and down. Move your hips with a wiggle and jiggle, a wiggle and jiggle, a wiggle and jiggle, and STOP. Sit very gently (crisscross, apple sauce, hands in your lap). Bear Lee will watch the most polite thinkers and not stinkers to see with whom he would like to come and sit today. While he watches, we will warm up our thinking.

WARM UP

Teacher says: Boys and girls, we will think of lots of ideas [**fluency**] about making wishes. Think about all the many wishes you could make. Think silently of as many ideas as you can while I time 60 seconds or 1 minute.....

As time ends, have students share one idea each until all the ideas are stated. No idea may be repeated during share time. Call attention to ideas that are **flexible**. For example if ideas have been toys, a bike, a Barbie doll, a Barbie house, etc., call attention to an idea such as, "my own bedroom so I don't have to share with my brother".

STORY TIME

Read the interactive story, *I Wish I Could, I Wish I Might, Have This Wish I Wish Tonight*. During the story, students will be asked to make predictions, create characters, and analyze pieces of the story. (Before reading the story, give each child a number card. During the story, the child who is holding the number in the blank will fill in the blank with his or her idea, thus completing a piece of the story. There are also questions along the way; let the students make predictions about what might happen next.

TIME TO CREATE

Following the story, allow students to go to a desk or table. Give them the star sheet (Appendix D). Say, "This is a wishing star; you will hide it in a picture by adding shapes and lines to transform it into something new and different. Use your star in a picture anyway you wish. You have only a few minutes to transform your star into something new [**originality**]." When time is up, have each child look at his/her picture. Tell them to look very carefully at the way they have used the star in a creative picture. Have them think of a title for the picture and label it [**elaborate**].

Each week, the teacher will take all the pictures and choose the most creative—the one with the most unique use of the shape into a new picture. Upon returning the following week, the children who have completed the most unique transformation will be awarded a creativity award (e.g., bear stickers, gummy bears, or bear cookies).

> I Wish I Could, I Wish I Might,
> Have This Wish I Wish Tonight

Bear Lee was an adorable bear. His hair was adorably soft. His eyes were adorably brown, and his parents thought he was absolutely adorable. As adorable as he was, Bear Lee was a bit adventuresome at times.

One night as he and his father were taking an evening walk, they saw a star falling from the sky.

Bear Lee's dad explained that it was really a meteorite which is a large rock-like thing. He explained further that when meteorites get close to the earth, the magnetic pull of earth's gravity pulls them down toward earth. And in the earth's atmosphere they burn on their way down, making them look like a "falling star." Then Bear Lee's dad said something very intriguing. He said that some people make a wish on falling stars.

Just then, Bear Lee made a wish that he would have pancakes dripping in his favorite honey for breakfast the next morning. The next day, he woke to the smell of sweet honey. To his delight, when he entered the kitchen, there sat his mom and dad with stacks of pancakes and the biggest jar of fresh honey his big brown eyes had ever beheld. Bear Lee decided this was his wish on a falling star come true.

That day, Bear Lee decided he would find another falling star, make another special wish. And how he wanted this wish more than anything in the world! His wish was _____ (**4, 8, 11, 19**).

So that very night, just as dark came, he climbed out his bedroom window to find another falling star upon which he could make a wish.

He walked along and walked along until he was deep in the darkness.

It was quiet at first, but as the darkness grew, he noticed noises all around. He thought the noises might be _____ (**5, 17, 20, 23**). When he looked closely in the direction of the sounds, he saw the crickets and frogs, but no falling stars.

He walked through some trees and felt a tickle. He thought the tickle was _____ (**9, 21, 22**). So, when the light from the moon trickled through the trees, he could see the wind was blowing leaves against his fury side. But he could still see no falling stars.

Just as he rounded the next tree, he saw something long and dark on the ground. "Oh my, I wonder what that could be," said

Bear Lee. He thought it might be _____ (**2, 6, 12, 16**). As he looked way up into the tree above, he saw an owl. With the moon in front of her, the owl's shadow was long on the ground. Still, as he looked beyond the owl, he saw no falling star.

Suddenly he said out loud, "I know, I must keep looking straight up so I won't miss any falling stars so I won't miss my wish. Up he looked as he continued his walk. But as he was looking up for falling stars, he wasn't looking down where his feet met _____ (**1, 3, 14, 18**). This made him go tumbling down, down, down the side of a hill.

As he landed on his back, he lay looking up at the night sky for a long time, but still he saw no falling stars. Bear Lee was growing very tired from his journey and search for a falling star upon which to make his special wish, _____ (**7, 10, 13, 15**). He started growing sleepy. Sometime later, he woke to the sounds of the night. He made his way home very sad that he had missed his chance to make a wish on a falling star.

Oh how good his bed felt; it even made his touch of sadness better as he drifted off to sleep.

The next morning as the sunshine warmed his face, he awoke to the sweet smell of honey which was waiting to be poured over breakfast – stacks and stacks of pancakes. As he entered the kitchen, his mom gave him the biggest bear hug and poured the honey deep over his stack of pancakes.

He got his wish after all!

OTHER QUESTIONS OR INQUIRY:

What was his wish?

How do you know?

Make a new ending for the story.

At the end of class, collect the creative work of all the children. The teachers should select the most unique creative picture/ transformation. For example: several children may use the star as a scene in the night sky. But the child who uses the star as a wheel on a vehicle, the body part of a prehistoric animal, or a scene at the end of a kaleidoscope, should be recognized as a creativity winner. Creativity winners might be recognized at the beginning of the next class with a sticker. Recommendations: This curriculum could be used in a study. Pretest students with a creativity measure that includes fluent, flexible, original, and elaborative processes. Engage the students in a series of lessons related to the sample lesson. Assess creative process following the conclusion of the lessons. See Appendix D for additional lesson activities for the unit "It's All About Bears."

Based on the documentation of students' creative thought and production, the chart should reveal a pattern showing which students are performing creatively on a consistent basis. In the event of repeated creativity, the child may be referred for assessment toward identification. The evidence collected through charting or documenting this performance-based creativity may be used in the total assessment case study.

A three year study (Milligan, 2009) was conducted using the C.R.E.A.T.E. model to determine if students in the primary grades could be recognized as creatively gifted through the documentation process. Kindergarten, first and second grade students from one school participated in lessons like the one presented in this chapter. Each child was given the Creativity Assessment Packet (CAP) Test of Divergent Thinking- Form A (Williams, 1993) during the 2005-06 school year before beginning the project. Over three years, the participant observer went into each classroom and presented lessons based on the model. One lesson was presented each week for the duration of the semester. While the lesson was being presented, classroom teachers documented exceptionally creative responses by the students. As each group exited the program, they were given the CAP Test of

Divergent Thinking—Form B (Williams, 1993). A comparison was made between the pre and post tests.

Over the course of three years, gains were made on the standardized test scores from the pre to post tests. The primary focus of this project, however, was to determine if a pattern emerged for exceptional creativity while children engaged in the activities. Patterns did emerge in the frequency of times particular students were documented exhibiting exceptionally creative responses and production. For example, of 20 children in one classroom, three of them (i.e., Ashley, Michael, and Shelly [pseudonyms]) were documented 6 to 8 times during 12 lessons as receiving creativity awards for transforming a shape into the most unique picture compared to classmates' ideas. Originality was rewarded (i.e., a sticker or gummy bear) on a weekly basis for creative expressions of original ideas.

Figure 7 is presented in order to provide a sample of the students' work and to demonstrate what constituted recognition for originality (i.e., creative expression of original ideas). At the end of one lesson, the students were given a circle and asked to transform it into a unique picture. Three of the children in the samples below used the circle as a face which was a common response among the children in the class (see sample 1, 2, and 3). One child (i.e., Shelly; see sample 4) transformed the circle into a cookie jar. This transformation was unique. When a child received recognition for creating something unique multiple times throughout the course of the semester, a pattern emerged on the chart documenting potential. It should also be noted that Toya and Sam (i.e., samples 2 and 3) were given a point or tally on the chart documenting elaboration for details in their transformations.

See Figure 7 to view the transformations.

During the collection of data for this project, some of the children emerged more competent to think of unique ideas and produce transformations exceptionally unique when compared to their age peers. Studying creativity in young children is a pursuit full of endless possibilities. We can be certain that all young children share some common traits in the realm of creative imagination and potential. We can be just as certain that a minority of

Figure 7
Transformations from One CREATE Lesson

Sample 1
Happy Face

Sample 2
Kitty

Sample 3
Alien

Sample 4
Cookie Jar – Yum

children in the primary grades possess creative abilities that exceed those of their age peers and require recognition in order to best serve the learning needs of those children. It is the responsibility of educators to provide the opportunities for the creative excellence to be shared and for the development of creative potential to emerge.

Consequently, it is the duty of all educators to provide a learning environment and opportunities for all children to express creativity. It was over 30 years ago that Paul Torrance (Rothenberg & Hausman, 1976) said it best:

> I am asked frequently if . . . recent studies advance us any further in the direction of a more creative kind of education than did Progressive Education. If one examines what we have learned . . . it should become evident that it is possible for us to advance . . . closer to achieving the American dream of a kind of education that will give every child a chance to grow and to achieve his creative potentialities. (p. 226)

Chapter 6

Cooperation With Classroom Teachers

Classroom teachers play an important role in the success of gifted programs. Over the past two decades, researchers (Bigelow, 1993; Bransky, 1987; Milligan, 2001; Tomlinson, 2001) consistently reported more support from classroom teachers for gifted programming when the teachers had a greater understanding of giftedness. On the other hand, when classroom teachers were unaware of characteristics of giftedness and appropriate programs for the gifted, the chances for successful identification of and service to the gifted children were greatly diminished (Starko, 1990).

Classroom Teacher's Knowledge of Giftedness

In a study by Starko (1990) teachers selected to implement enrichment and acceleration strategies reported that they were told they would provide programming for gifted students. The reason for their selection, given by the administrators, was because those teachers were creative, young, and or "gung ho." One teacher stated, "When I said I didn't know what I was doing, they said, You decide!" (Starko, 1990, p. 35). Another teacher said, "I knew nothing. I had no preparation. Nobody sent me anywhere. Nobody gave me any clues" (Starko, 1990, p. 35).

According to the classroom teachers who were made responsible for providing services to gifted children, the school district was unable to maintain a program for the gifted due to a lack of teacher preparation and knowledge about giftedness.

Hickey (1990) also studied classroom teachers' perceptions of giftedness and appropriate programming for the gifted. In the study, 27 teachers were surveyed and asked to identify major problems related to gifted programs and make recommendations regarding services for gifted students. Classroom teachers from the study described problems with gifted programming in the following areas: (a) disruptions caused by gifted students being pulled from class for program services, (b) conflicts that existed in opinions about the definition of giftedness, (c) complaints by teachers and other students that program participants behaved arrogantly, and (d) complaints by teachers and parents that tracking was detrimental to lower performing students. Hickey also reported that when teachers lacked training related to gifted children, they were less likely to make accommodations in the classroom to differentiate curriculum for the gifted.

Recommendations for improving gifted programs were also made by teachers in Hickey's study. The recommendations included the following: (a) using models besides pull-out programming, (b) employing better screening procedures to help insure that only the truly gifted were served, (c) providing an "elective period" during the school day when students could attend special classes so that supplemental materials could be utilized for the rest of the class at the same time, (d) stressing that gifted means different not better, and (e) providing better communications and planning between the classroom teacher and the teacher of gifted students.

An important relationship between the Starko (1990) and Hickey (1990) studies exists. In both studies, teachers' understanding of giftedness was vital in the successful programming for gifted children. Also, from both studies, classroom teachers could not assist with identifying gifted students if they did not know how. And when classroom teachers felt left out because a specialist was the only one making decisions about placement and programming for the gifted, there was a lack of continuity in curriculum between the gifted program and the regular classroom. Diezsi and Cummings (1987) gave as an example of bad management of communication: "Make it the sole province of one 'very special' teacher. Then make it clear that everyone else should keep hands off" (p. 27). In 2008 (Milligan) interviews were conducted with approximately 200 classroom teachers to assess and compare their knowledge of (a) characteristics of giftedness, (b) identification procedures for their school district and (c) strategies for differentiating curriculum for the gifted.

Eighty-nine percent of the classroom teachers interviewed reported that gifted students are those who make all A's, are highly motivated, are self-directed, and are outgoing. While this does fit the profile or many gifted children, not all gifted children are perfect students (Hertzog & Robinson, 2005; VanTassel-Baska, 2006). Educators of the gifted may also assume that classroom teachers understand the identification process. However, fifteen percent of the teachers interviewed reported understanding the identification procedures. Those who understood kinds of assessment instruments used to determine potential and ability had previously served on identification committees. Those same teachers were the ones who knew what kinds of criteria were used to place students in the program for the gifted. In the interviews, only 8% of the classroom teachers reported awareness of the GT Frameworks used by the facilitator of the gifted for program planning and services. Approximately 12% reported the use of some varied or different teaching strategies for those who were identified as gifted, talented, or creative.

These statistics are especially disconcerting when we consider the root of many misconceptions by classroom teachers—lack of communication between the specialist for gifted education and other teachers. When programs are structured so that gifted children are with a specialist for only a few hours a week and the remaining time educational needs are being met in the regular classroom, the need for collaboration is apparent.

In more positive terms, Diezsi and Cummings (1987) also reported successful participation of classroom teachers in implementing services for gifted children when teachers were involved in (a) creating gifted characteristic checklists, (b) coordinating program services, (c) designing courses to meet the needs of the gifted, and (d) conferencing with parents about gifted students.

Drawn from research finding and expert opinion, it is concluded that the classroom teacher's knowledge about giftedness and involvement in curriculum planning for gifted children are important to the success of gifted programs. Promising practices for classroom teachers and successful gifted education begins with a cooperation between the educator of gifted children and the classroom teacher.

In a study conducted by Milligan and Campbell and Milligan (2003), teachers of a summer program for gifted students reported the positive effects of communication and co-teaching. These teachers said that as they shared rooms and did team teaching, a sense of camaraderie and security developed. They also said that sharing ideas during planning made the co-teaching more than just the shared teaching of a lesson. The experience became a source of shared decision-making and professional growth for all participants.

Continued findings (Bangel, Enersen, Capobianco, and Moon, 2006) indicated the positive impact of staff development on classroom teachers' awareness and concern for gifted learners. A cohort of preservice teachers was assessed prior to a practicum. Interviews, classroom observations, and lesson planning were used to evaluate the preservice teachers' perceptions of giftedness. At the end of the practicum, it was reported that an increased level of knowledge and preparation improved their comfort level and confidence to identify and teach the gifted in their future classrooms.

Educating Classroom Teachers Through Staff Development

Knowing which students to recommend for assessment toward identification of giftedness is based on a teacher's knowledge of what giftedness means. Teachers' knowledge about giftedness may be enhanced through staff development. Staff development was described by Orlich (1989) as a global plan with a specific process: "protected under its umbrella are all inservice education activities or projects" (p. 7). The goal of staff development should be to provide guidance for teachers in order that they achieve a long-range working model. Dettmer (1990) confirmed the distinction between staff development and inservice training in a manner similar to Orlich's (1980). Both authors' recommendations for staff development included the following: (a) inservice training to expand knowledge and increase teacher effectiveness; (b) organization planning to improve programming and solve problems; (c) consultation in the form of workshops, inservice clinics, and special projects; (d) provisions for resources, coordination, and assistance with inter-building communications; (e) assistance with researching, implementing, and evaluating new practices and procedures; and (f) evaluation of staff development efforts and organizing feedback.

Inservice training as one component of staff development has been an established tradition in the education profession; thousands of papers have been written about the most and least effective types of inservice. Related literature distinguished inservice training as it pertained to skills taught in the regular classroom and curriculum for gifted children. Tomlinson (2001) reported that teachers who attended inservice training about giftedness preferred (a) active participation in the discussion, (b) handouts with activities to use in their classrooms, (c) visuals to explain information, and (d) techniques for implementing ideas and materials. The least effective types of inservice were lecture, sessions with equipment problems, and occasions when there was personal dislike for the speaker's attitude about gifted education.

So who is responsible for educating classroom teachers about the assessment of giftedness and appropriate services? You are! As the specialists for gifted education, you have an obligation to present staff development to classroom teachers so they can help you identify the gifted and offer differentiated curriculum to them in the classroom.

By defining staff development in global terms, educators of gifted children have an obligation to offer staff development sessions which inform teachers of (a) the characteristics of giftedness, (b) the assessment procedures, and (c) the identification process. For staff development, GTC teachers have an obligation to model to classroom teachers ways to serve gifted children in the classroom also.

Suggestions for Telling Others About Giftedness

There are several strategies that may be implemented to make staff development with classroom teachers productive for all involved. Suggestions are illustrated in Figure 8.

Just as there are some strategies in general regarding appropriate staff development, there are some strategies for effective inservice. These suggestions include: (a) make it interactive; (b) be concise; (c) let the audience draw some conclusions; (d) let them know you are always looking for suggestions; and (e) leave them in the spirit of cooperation. Specifically, make it interactive by perhaps beginning the session with an activity that allows the participants a couple of minutes to work in groups listing characteristics of giftedness. Then have them share their answers around the room until all the ideas have been stated. Be concise with the information. Extensive information about administration guidelines, scoring procedures, or statistical information about the identification procedure is unnecessary. Let them draw some conclusions by asking them if they feel students in their classroom have been accurately identified. Let them know you welcome their suggestions for ways to identify giftedness. Leave time at the end of the presentation to take their questions. And leave them in the spirit of cooperation by telling them to call you for assistance. Figure 9 illustrates ways to give the information at the inservice session long and active life.

Positive Influence

Staff development for classroom teachers about giftedness can occur in several forms. Informally, teachers of the gifted may dis-

Figure 8
Informing Classroom Teachers About Identification of Giftedness

STAFF DEVELOPMENT OF CLASSROOM TEACHERS
REGARDING GIFTEDNESS

- Present a 20 to 30 minute inservice at a faculty meeting at the beginning of the school year.

- Invite an expert guest speaker from a university, nearby educational cooperative, or school district to present.

- Have a year-end meeting with all classroom teachers to receive feedback on the year's efforts to make GT identification and services a a cooperative effort.

- Do co-teaching with classroom teachers to demonstrate "enrichment." Incorporate basic skills or standards from the classroom teacher's curriculum

- Go to the playground during the teacher's recess duty. Help him/her with duty while discussing nominations of students to the program.

- Provide a newsletter, periodic updates, and information to all teachers regarding program events or current issues in gifted education.

- Invite classrooms to attend state meetings and conferences related to gifted children.

cuss assessment procedures and prospective nomination of students. Teachers of the gifted may offer staff development by conducting demonstration lessons while classroom teachers document potential giftedness. Formal staff development may occur in the form of inservice. It is the responsibility of the teacher or administrator of the gifted to provide classroom teacher training.

Figure 9
Making A Lasting Impression

Prepare & Share
MAKING INSERVICE LAST

Brochure   Describe what you're going to present.

Hand-outs   Provide information (e.g., a list of characteristics, identification, program options, etc.).

Pamphlets   Describe the identification procedure and program services.

Scrapbooks   A picture is worth a thousand words.

Visuals   Use transparencies, power point, or poster board sharing activities and projects completed by gifted children.

Evidence is abundant and logic suggests that classroom teachers need professional development to better understand and serve giftedness. One study (Milligan, 2001) revealed that each teacher in grades K–4 changed something about the way he or she defined giftedness, and they each increased the number of students they nominated for assessment following a year-long systematic plan for staff development. The staff development included demonstration lessons presented by the facilitator of gifted children and four formal inservice sessions presented by a variety of speakers.

Building good public relations may be one of the most important roles of the facilitator or administrator of gifted children. The more comfortable classroom teachers feel working as a team and the more teachers know as a result of effective professional development, the better the chance for accurate identification. And working together with parents, teachers, administrators, and counselors will increase the chance of better serving gifted children.

Chapter 7

Pulling It All Together

Using Profile Data

In the previous chapters, appropriate procedures and assessment instruments have been reviewed. We have also discussed assessment of subpopulations, assessment of students in the primary grades, and assessment with the assistance of classroom teachers. The *identification* process was described in the following terms: (a) the *nomination* or screening of students with high achievement test scores, (b) the notification to parents to obtain *permission to test*, (c) the administration of *assessment instruments* (typically measures of cognitive, verbal, and creative abilities), (d) the use of any *checklists* by teachers or parents for motivation, task commitment, leadership, or talents, and/or (e) the inclusion of *subjective evidence* or nontraditional measures (for example, portfolio samples, products, creative production). Variations of this process exist among school districts and from state to state. But the more comprehensive the assessment process, the more the likelihood of accurate placement of students is enhanced.

The compilation of data into an understandable and concise context is the next challenge. This author recommends placing data such as test scores on a profile or data form so that scores can be interpreted comparatively. In other terms, when exceptional abstract thinking, creativity, standardized test scores, motivation, leadership, and the like are used to identify giftedness, scores can be listed (and charted) according to percentile ranks. The use of percentile ranks for scores on each assessment instrument of the checklist makes the listing and comparison of scores easy to follow. The use of a profile form for such information provides a visual depiction of a student's scores. Another advantage to listing scores and percentile ranks is that most assessment instruments, whether IQ tests, creativity assessments, or checklists, have a manual that converts raw scores to a percentile rank. Portfolio samples, pictures of products, or other evidence of creative production may be attached to the student profile. See Figure 9, Student Profile, which provides a sample of various assessment instruments used to identify gifted students.

A Committee's Decision

Typically, a committee composed of at least one specialist in gifted education, a counselor, a variety of classroom teachers, and an administrator review the student profiles for placement. The facilitator of gifted children may be required by the school district to train others on the characteristics, assessment measures, and qualification of students for placement. Notice that on the Student Profile in Figure 11, there is no place on the form for the student's name. The child's identity should be unknown to the committee in order to minimize the chance for bias on the part of any committee member.

In training professionals to represent the school district as members of the identification or placement committee, a brief inservice session on the instruments used, the interpretation of scores, and the criteria used by the state or school district to define giftedness is recommended. There is some important information all committee members need to have: (a) Gifted chil-

Figure 10
Sample Student Profile Sheet for Assessment Data

STUDENT PROFILE
Talents and Gifts (TAG)

Submitted by:_____Grade:_____

Percentile ranks or Percentages	Poor 2–39	Average 40–74	Good 75–89	Excellent 90–99
K – Bit (IQ Assessment) Verbal				
Matrices/ Abstract Thinking				
Composite				
Williams CAP Creative Thinking				
Creative Feeling				
Parent Rating				
Stanford 9 Achievement Total Language				
Total Math				
Highest Area				
_____ Total Battery				
Renzulli Rating Scale Learning Characteristics				
Leadership				
Motivation				

Comments:
_____

_____

_____

Placement Recommendation ____P.   ____N.P.   Code_____

P = Placed   (See attached portfolio samples, pictures
N.P. = Not Placed   of products, or other evidence of
                        creative production.)

dren are not necessarily gifted in all academic content, (b) highly creative and intellectual children may not make straight A's, and (c) when the majority of the scores from assessment instruments fall within the 95th percentile and above, there is sufficient evidence for placement.

Figure 10 is an example of student scores. Notice that even though the scores for abstract thinking, creative feeling, mathematics, and leadership are in the "good" range rather than "exceptional," the committee has recommended placement of child in the program, which serves giftedness.

Another frequently used method for review of test scores and student production is to rank order Student Profiles according to the most outstanding (i.e., highest scores in the greatest number of categories). Each committee member reviews the student information. If there are 12 students under consideration for placement, each committee member gives each profile a number ranking, 1 through 12. The score of 1 goes to the student profile the committee member feels is the most qualified for program services—that is, the student who has the highest scores across the greatest number of categories. The student with the next highest scores across the board would be given a 2, and so on. The committee chair (typically, the coordinator of the program for gifted children) compiles the rankings of all committee members to determine which students are ranked the highest by majority opinion. Those students will be placed into the program for the gifted contingent upon parental permission to participate. This system is sometimes used when a state allocates funds for 5% of the student population. The identification committee would be limited on the number of students recommended for program services.

There are, however, drawbacks to this method. When identification committee meetings occur several times in one school year, there is no consistent means of insuring the same criteria applies to student placement at the various meetings. What may be a top ranked student compared to her/his peers at one meeting, might not rank as high at the next meeting if compared to another group of peers. Also, there is no way to accommodate

Figure 11
Profile of Student Scores

STUDENT PROFILE
Talents and Gifts (TAG)

Submitted by:_____Grade:_____

Percentile ranks or Percentages	Poor 2–39	Average 40–74	Good 75–89	Excellent 90–99
K – Bit (IQ Assessment) Verbal				√
Matrices/ Abstract Thinking			√	
Composite				√
Williams CAP Creative Thinking				√
Creative Feeling			√	
Parent Rating				√
Stanford 9 Achievement Total Language				√
Total Math			√	
Highest Area _____				√
Total Battery				√
Renzulli Rating Scale Learning Characteristics				√
Leadership			√	
Motivation				√

Comments:
_____

_____

Placement Recommendation ___√__P.   ____N.P.   Code_____
                                                  (See attached portfolio samples, pictures
P. = Placed   of products, or other evidence of
N.P. = Not Placed   creative production.)

ratings for various grade levels. For example, in the primary grades different methods of assessment may be used from those for the intermediate grades. A discrepancy in assessment methods might be advantageous for one group or another in rankings by committee members.

Contacting the Parents

Upon agreement by the committee to place a child in the program that serves the learning needs of gifted children, the student's parents must consent to the placement of the child. A sample parent letter for placement is included as Figure 12.

We hope all children who are nominated and tested qualify for program services according to the identification committee's recommendation. However, the reality is that not all children who are nominated will be placed. Parents must be notified just the same. A sample letter may be seen in Figure 13.

Conferencing with the Parents

Telling parents their child has been identified for placement in a program which serves giftedness is easy. They are usually excited and proud that their child has been recognized as "gifted." But whether the conference has been scheduled to discuss the need for program services by a facilitator of the gifted or to discuss the need for the child to remain in the regular classroom, the news to the parents is to *focus on meeting the child's learning needs*. Further, there are some general rules for effective parent conferences that may be beneficial to educators of the gifted.

An article by Quiroz (1999) describes the importance of bridging cultures with parent-teacher conferences. According to the

Figure 12
Sample Parent Letter for Placement

Pleasant School District
1200 Pleasant Dr.
Goodville, MS 77880
(456) 789-1234

Dear [Mr./Mrs./Ms.] _____,

Recently, you received a letter and consent form to test your daughter Maria for the TAG program. A case study was compiled using IQ tests, creativity assessments, standardized achievement test scores, rating scales, and portfolio samples. Following the compilation of scores, a committee reviewed the case study data. The committee recommended that Maria be placed in the program, which serves the learning needs of gifted children.

We wish to request a conference with you in order to discuss (a) Maria's case study, (b) program service options, (c) the management plan to differentiate curriculum, and (d) to secure your signature on the placement form. Please contact Ms. Doe at the number or address in the letterhead above to schedule a conference at your convenience.

Thank you in advance for your help. We look forward to meeting you.

Sincerely,

Jane Doe
TAG Coordinator

Figure 13
Sample Parent Letter for Continuation in the Regular Classroom

Pleasant School District
1200 Pleasant Dr.
Goodville, MS 77880
(456) 789-1234

Dear [Mr./Mrs./Mrs. _____],

Recently, we wrote to you to tell you that your daughter Maria was under consideration for the TAG program. At that time, you gave us permission to give her some tests. A case study was compiled using IQ tests, creativity assessments, standardized achievement test scores, rating scales, and portfolio samples. Following the compilation of scores, a committee reviewed the case study data (no names were attached to any of that information). The committee recommended that Maria's learning needs would best be met in the regular classroom at this time.

We'd like to have a conference with you to discuss Maria's case study and the particular abilities that it seems to direct attention to, as well as our various educational programs. Please contact Ms. Doe at the number or address listed above to schedule a conference at your convenience.

Thank you in advance for your help. We look forward to meeting you.

Sincerely,

Jane Doe
TAG Coordinator

author, there are some important beginning or prerequisite steps to effective dialog with parents. These include (a) understanding backgrounds, (b) being honest with parents and (c) being a good listener.

Other authors (Benson, 1999; Robinson, 1997) agree on some common factors toward making parent conferences positive interactions. Teachers can improve the chances for a successful conference by (a) laying the groundwork for positive relations on the phone, (b) conducting the conference with open lines of communication, (c) including the student in the conference when possible, and (d) making the meeting comfortable for all involved.

Now, specifically how do these strategies apply to the conference with parents of a child who have just received a letter saying that their child did not qualify for program services for gifted education? First, when the conference date is established, inform the parents that you will provide them a copy of the scores from the assessments you administered and that you will give them some materials for enhancing and developing their child's potential. This information indicates you are going to share informative and helpful information. You particularly want to convey the message that the school will continue to be aware of and alert to their child as an individual.

When the parents arrive, and following proper introductions, have materials available, laid out, and ready to share. Remind the parents that a variety of assessment instruments were used to make a decision about the best and most appropriate placement of the child. Show the parents the profile sheet while explaining that a committee reviewed the data. Explain that the process is bias-free since the committee members see no names of the children. Inform them that the identification committee is trained to place children whose scores fall within the 95th percentile and above on the majority of the categories on the Student Profile. Have a copy of the Student Profile sheet ready for the parents along with materials (an article from professional literature, a list of resources, web sites explaining exceptional potential, etc.) you plan to give them.

Throughout the conference, welcome questions. Be prepared for questions pertaining to additional ways to assess giftedness, questions about the possibility of having their child nominated and tested again, and questions about how to tell their child they will not be receiving direct services without damaging self-esteem. Of all the questions, the later will be the most important to address. Some recommended resources for facilitators of gifted kids and the person in charge of conferencing with parents follow.

When opportunity and personnel are available to include students who are nominated but do not qualify for program service, a "talent pool" is a good way to serve their learning needs. Talent pools are established in a variety of ways. But ultimately, the students with high potential or are academically advanced, have the opportunity to participate in activities that challenge and enhance their talents. A list of websites about talent pools are listed in Table 11.

The responsibility of properly identifying students for placement in programs for the gifted is enormous. The process is contingent upon proper selection of assessment instruments and procedures. It is a cooperative effort between classroom teachers, parents, counselors, administrators, and the teacher or administrator of the gifted that make the process successful. The ultimate benefit is appropriately meeting the learning needs of our gifted, talented, and creative youth.

Table 11

Web sites About The Use of Talent Pools for Students Who Don't Qualify for Direct Services

Web site	Description
www.etown.k12.ky.us	Elizabethtown Independent School District has a **Talent Pool** for grades K–3.
www.lawrence.k12.ky.us	Grades 1–4 are served in a **Talent Pool.**
www.hapton.k12.wi.us	This **Talent Pool** is designed to meet the needs of high potential students.
www.hssd.k12.va.us	Talent Pool and gifted services are utilized here.
http://www.hssd.k12.wi.us/gifted1.htm	The Howard-Suamico School District has a Gifted and Talented program that serves 40% of the students in a **Talent Pool.**
www.ahs.k12.wi.us	Any student who is accepted into an Honors class becomes a member of the "**Gifted** and Talented **Talent Pool.**"

References

Abell, D., & Lennex, L. (1999). *Gifted education: Don't overlook the disadvantaged.* Point Clear, AL: Mid-South Educational Research Association. (ERIC Document Reproduction Service No. ED 436 918)

Aschbacher, P. R., & Winters, L. (1992). *A practical guide to alternative assessment.* Alexandria, VA: Association for Supervision and Curriculum Development.

Bangel, N. J., Enersen, D., Capobianco, B., & Moon, S. M. (2006). Professional development of preservice teachers: Teaching in the super Saturday program. *Journal for the Education of the Gifted.* 29(3), 339-361.

Bennett, G. K. (1982). *Differential aptitude test.* San Antonio, TX: Harcourt Brace Educational Measurement.

Benson, B. (1999). *Student-led conferencing using showcase portfolios.* Thousand Oaks, CA: Corwin Press.

Bigelow, R. (1993). *Developing and implementing a program to improve school success for minority students.* Nova University: Practicum Report. (ERIC Document Reproduction Service No. ED 365 007)

Binet, A. (1905). New methods for the diagnosis of the intellectual level of subnormals. *L'Ann'ee Psychologique*, 12, 191–244.

Bracken, B. A., & McCallum, S. R. (1997). *Universal nonverbal intelligence test.* Chicago, IL: Riverside Publishing.

Bransky, T. (1987). Specific program information: A key to attitudes about the gifted education. *Gifted Child Quarterly, 31*(1), 29–32.

Bull, K. S. (1988). Rural gifted education: An introduction. *Rural Special Education Quarterly,8*(4), 2–4.

Cassell, R. N. (1965) *Leadership Q-Sort Test.* Murfreesboro, TN: Psychometric Affiliates.

Cattell, K., & Cattell, R. (1965). *Culture fair intelligence test.* Champaign, IL: Institute for Personality and Ability Testing Inc.

Clark, B. (1992). *Growing up gifted.* Columbus, OH: Macmillan.

Coleman, M. R., & Gallagher, J. (1995). State identification policies: Gifted students from special populations. *Roeper Review, 17*(4), 268–275.

Cross, T. L., & Dixon, F. A. (1998). On gifted students in rural schools. *Education for the Gifted and Talented*

Cross, T. L., & Stewart, R. (1995). A phenomenological investigation of the Lebenswelt of gifted students in rural high schools. *Journal of Secondary Gifted Education, 6,* 273–280.

Davidson, K. L. (1992). A comparison of Native American and white students' cognitive strengths as measured by the Kaufman Assessment Battery for Children. *Roeper Review, 14*(3), 111–114.

Deal, V. R., & Yan, M. (1985). Resource guide to multicultural tests and materials. *Asha 27*(6), 43–49.

Dettmer, P. (1990). *Staff development for gifted programs.* National Association for Gifted Children: Washington, D. C.

Diezsi, C. P., & Cummings, W. B. (1987). This gifted program enriches teachers as well as students. *Executive Educator, 9*(2), 27–29.

Edwin, F. (1978). *Leadership Opinion Questionnaire.* Chicago, IL: Reid London House.

Feldhusen, J., & Clinkenbeard, P. (1986). Creativity instructional materials: A review of research. *Journal of Creative Behavior, 20,* 176–188.

Feldman, D. H. (1982). *Developmental approaches to giftedness and creativity: New directions for child development.* San Francisco, CA: Jossey-Bass.

Ford, D. Y. (1994). Nurturing resilience in gifted black youth. *Roeper Review,* 17(2), 80–85.

Frasier, M., (1991). Disadvantaged and culturally diverse gifted students. *Journal for the Education of the Gifted, 14,* 234–245.

Galton, Francis (1869). *Hereditary genius.* New York: Macmillan.

Gagne, F. (1995). Hidden meaning of the "talent development" concept. *The Educational Forum, 59*(4), 350–362.

Gardner, H. (1983). *Frames of mind.* New York: Basic Books.

Gear, G. H. (1984). Providing services for rural gifted children. *Exceptional Children, 50*(4), 326–331.

Gilliam, J. E., Carpenter, B. D., & Christensen, J. R. (1996). *Gifted and talented evaluation scales.* Austin, TX: Pro-Ed.

Hatch, T. & Gardner, H. (1988, November/December). New research on intelligence, *Learning,* pp. 36–39.

Hertzog, C., & Robinson, A. E. (2005). Metacognition and intelligence. In O. Wilhelm & R. W. Engle (Eds.) *Understanding and measuring intelligence.* London: Sage, 101–123.Hertzog, 2005.

Hickey, M. G. (1990). Classroom teachers' concerns and recommendations for improvement of gifted programs, *Roeper Review,* 12(4), 265–267.

Hollingworth, L. (1942). *Children above 180 IQ.* New York: World Book.

Howley, A. A., Pendarvis, E. D., & Howley, C. B. (1988). Gifted students in rural environments: Implication for school programs. *Rural Special Education Quarterly, 8*(4), 43–50.

Howley, C. (1994). *The academic effectiveness of small-scale schooling.* (An Update) (ERIC Document Reproduction Service No. ED 372 897).

Johnsen, S., & Corn, A. (1992). *Screening assessment for gifted elementary students.* Austin, TX: Pro-Ed. Inc.

Karnes, F., & Chauvin, J. C. (2000). *Leadership skills inventory.* Scottsdale, AZ: Gifted Psychology Press.

Kaufman, A. S., & Kaufman, N. L. (2004). *Kaufman brief intelligence test–2.* Cycle Pine, MN: American Guidance Services.

Kingore, B. W. (1990). *The Kingore observation inventory (KOI).* Des Moines, IO: Learderhip Publishers Inc.

Kingore, B. W. (2001). *The Kingore observation inventory: Second edition.* Austin, TX: Professional Associates Publishing.

Kite, E. S. (1916). *The development of intelligence in children.* Vineland, NJ: Publications for the Training School in Vineland.

Lewis, J. D. (2000). *Rural gifted education, enhancing service delivery.* Alexandria, VA: Capitalizing on Leadership in Rural Special Education. (ERIC Document Reproduction Service No. ED 439 874)

Lohman, D., & Hagen, E. (2000). *Cognitive abilities test.* Chicago, IL: Riverside Publishing Co.

Marland, S. (1971). *Education of the gifted and talented: Report to the Congress of the United States by the U. S. Commissioner of Education.* Washington, DC: U.S. Government Printing Office.

McGre, K., & Mather, N. (2003). Woodcock-Johnson III tests of cognitive abilities. Chicago, IL: Riverside Publishing.

Meeker, M., & Meeker, R. (1975). *Structure of the intellect abilities test: Screen for a-typical gifted.* Vida, OR: SOI Systems.

Miller, B. S. (1981). Gifted children and their families. In B. S. Miller & M. Price (Eds.), *The gifted child, the family, and the community.* New York: Walker & Co.

Milligan, J. (2001). Effective staff development in a low socio-economic rural setting: A microethnography of teacher's perceptions of giftedness. (ERIC Document Reproduction Service No. ED 450 992)

Milligan, J., & Campbell, D. (2003). It's a fit: Collaboration and gifted education. *Understanding Our Gifted, 15*(3), 18–21.

Milligan, J. (2008). Classroom teachers: It matters what they know about gifted matters. *Understanding Our Gifted,* 20(3), 18-21.

Milligan, J. (2009). Discovering exceptional creative potential of children in primary grades using the C.R.E.A.T.E. model. *Perspectives In Gifted Education.* University of Denver: CO, Vol. 5, 118-143.

Naglieri, J. A. (1996). *Naglieri nonverbal ability tests individual administration.* San Antonio, TX: The Psychological Corporation.

Nelson, G. J., & French, J. L. (1973). *Henmon-Nelson test of mental ability.* Chicago, IL: Riverside Publishing Co.

Nelson, R., & McCann, C. (1989). *The at-risk student.* Publication for the College of Education. Conway, AR: University of Central Arkansas.

Orlich, D. C. (1989). *Staff development: Enhancing human potential.* Needham Heights, MA: Allyn and Bacon.

Osborn, A. (1963). *Applied imagination (3rd ed.).* New York: Charles Scribner.

Otis, A., & Lennon, R. (1967). *Otis-Lennon school mental ability test.* San Antonio, TX: Harcourt Brace Educational Measurement.

Passow, H., & Rudnitski, R. (1993). *State policies regarding education of the gifted as reflected in legislation and regulation.* Collaborative Research Study CRS93302. Storrs, CT: National Research Center on the Gifted and Talented.

Pfeiffer, S. I. (2003). Challenges and opportunities for students who are gifted: What the experts say. *The Gifted Child Quarterly, 47*(2) p. 161–166.

Piaget, J. (1952). *The origin of intelligence in children.* New York: International Universities Press.

Piirto, J. (1999). *Talented children and adults: Their development and education.* Upper Saddle River, NJ: Prentice Hall.

Plucker, J., & McIntire, J. (1996). Academic survivability in high potential, middle school students. *Gifted Child Quarterly 40,* 7–14.

Quiroz, B. (1999). Bridging cultures with parent-teacher conference. *Educational Leadership (56)* 68–70.

Raven, J. C., & Court, J. H. (1995). *Raven's progressive matrices.* New York: Psychological Corporation.

Renzulli, J. (1986). The three-ring conception of giftedness: A developmental model for creative productivity. In R. J. Sternberg & J. E. Davidson (Eds.), *Conceptions of giftedness* (pp. 53–92). Cambridge, U.K.: Cambridge University Press.

Renzulli, J. S., Smith, L. H., White, A. J., & Callahan, C. M., & Hartman, R. K. & Westburg, K. L. (2002). *Scales for rating the behavioral characteristics of superior students.* Mansfield Center, CT: Creative Learning Press.

Richert, S. E. (1987). Rampant problems and promising practices in the identification of disadvantaged gifted students. *Gifted Child Quarterly, 31*(4), 149–154.

Robinson, S. L. (1997). Parent conference tips *Teaching PreK–8, 28,* 78.

Roid, G. H. (2003). *Stanford-Binet* (5th ed.). Chicago, IL: Riverside Publishing.

Sashkin, M., (2001). *Leadership behavior questionnaire.* San Francisco, CA: Berrett-Koehler Publications.

Shaklee, B., Whitmore, J., Barton, L., Barbour, N., Ambrose, R., & Viechnicki, K. (1989). *Early assessment for exceptional potential for young and/or economically disadvantaged students.* Washington, DC: Office of Educational Research Grant No. R206A00160.

Slosson, R., Nicholson, C., & Hibpshman, T. (1996). *Slosson intelligence test.* East Aurora, NY: Slosson Educational Publication, Inc.

Smutny, J. F. (2003). *Designing and developing programs for gifted students*. Thousand Oaks, CA: Corwin Press, Inc.Smutny, J. F. (2003). *Designing and developing programs for gifted students*. Thousand Oaks, CA: Corwin Press, Inc.

Smutny, J. F., & Blocksom, R. H. (1990). *Education of the gifted*. Bloomington, IN: Phi Delta Kappa Educational Foundation.

Spicker, J. P., Southern, D., & Davis B. I. (1987). The rural gifted child. *Gifted Child Quarterly, 3* (4), 155–157.

South, J., (1971). Gifted children among minority groups: A crying need for recognition. *Top of the News, (28)* 43–48.

Starko, A. J. (1990). Life and death of a gifted program: Lessons not yet learned. *Roeper Review, 13*(1), 33–38.

Sternberg, R. (1988). *The triarchic mind: A new theory of human intelligence*. New York: Viking.

Tannenbaum, (1983). *Gifted children: Psychological and educational perspectives*. New York: Macmillian.

Terman, L. (1925). *Mental and physical traits of a thousand gifted children*. Stanford, CA: Stanford University Press.

Terman, L., & Oden, M. H. (1959). *The gifted child grows up*. Stanford, CA: Stanford University Press.

Terman, L. (1969). Intelligence and its measurement: A symposium. In L. E. Tyler (Eds.), *Intelligence: Some recurring issues* (pp. 3–25). New York: Van Nostrand Reinhold Company.

Terman, L. (1975). *The discovery and encouragement of exceptional talent*. In W. B. Barbe & J. S. Renzulli (Eds.), New York: Irvington.

Tomlinson, (2001). Differentiated instruction in the regular classroom: What does it mean? How does it look? *Understanding Our Gifted, 14*(1), 3–6.

Torrance, E. P. (1962). *Guiding creative talent*. Englewood Cliffs, NJ: Prentice-Hall.

Torrance, E. P. (1977). *Creativity in the classroom*. Washington, DC: National Education Association.

Torrance, E. P. (1987). Teaching for creativity. In S. Isaksen (Ed.), *Frontiers of creativity research: Beyond the basics* (pp. 190–215). Buffalo: Bearly Ltd.

Torrance, P. (2008). *Torrance test of creative thinking: Norms-technical manual, Figural (Streamline) Forms A & B.* Bensenville, IL: Scholastic Testing Service.

Treffinger, D. J. (1987). Research on creativity. *Gifted Child Quarterly, 30*(1), 15–19.

Valencia, A. A. (1985). Curriculum perspectives for gifted limited-English-proficient students. *The Journal for the National Association for Bilingual Education*, 10(1), 65–77.

VanTassel-Baska (2002). Using performance tasks in the identification of economically disadvantaged and minority gifted learners: Findings from project STAR. *Gifted Child Quarterly,* 46(2), 110-123.

VanTassel-Baska, (2006) *Serving Gifted Learners Beyond the Traditional Classroom: A Guide to Alternative Programs and Services*, Prufrock Press, Waco, TX.

Wechsler, D. (2003). *Wechsler intelligence scale – 4th edition.* New York: Psychological Corporation.

Wechsler, D. (2003). *Wechsler preschool and primary scale of intelligence – revised.* New York: Psychological Corporation.

Williams, F. (1993). *Creativity assessment packet.* Austin, TX: Pro-Ed., Inc.

Witty, P. (1958). The gifted child. Boston: D. C. Heath & Co.

Wolf, T. H. (1973). *Alfred Binet.* Chicago, IL: University of Chicago Press.

Woodcock, R. W., McGree, K. & Mather, N. (2003). *Woodcock-Johnson Tests of Cognitive Ability.* Itasca, IL: Riverside Publishing, A Houghton Mifflin Company.

Definitions of Assessment Terms

Assessment: A process involving observation, collection of data, and the interpretation of information to measure learner success or ability. Assessment can be achieved through interviews, rating scales, checklists, inventories, and tests.

Alternative Assessment: An alternative to traditional standardized, norm or criterion referenced, or pencil and paper tests.

Authentic Assessment: Evaluating by asking for the behaviors the learner is intended to produce. Tasks used in authentic assessment are meaningful and valuable, and part of the learning process. Examples include open-ended responses, working out a solution to a problem, producing work or a task, portfolios or observation.

Benchmark: Student performance standards based on competences in a content area which are checked at various points through the learning process.

Evaluation: Qualitative and quantitative measures of the learner's performance. A collection of information or assessments to make informed decisions about continued instruction.

I.Q. Test: A standardized, norm-referenced test used as a measurement of general intelligence. It measures analytical skills and cognitive performance (e.g., memory, perception, abstract reasoning).

Mean: Figured by adding all the scores of a group and dividing by the number of test-takers. The calculated number is the mean score.

Median: The point on a scale that divides a group into two equal subgroups. An equal number of scores fall above the median and below the median.

Norm Group: A random selected group selected to take a test in order to establish the range of scores by percentile.

Normal Curve Equivalent: A score that ranges from 1–99, used to compare different tests for the same student or group of students. An NCE is a normalized test score with a mean of 50 and a standard deviation of 21.06.

Percentile: A ranking scale from low (1) to high (99) with 50 as the median score. A percentile rank indicates the percentage of the norm group scores compared to the score of the test taker. In other words, to score at the 70th percentile means that 70 percent of the people in the norm group scored at or below the test-taker's score.

Portfolio Assessment: Samples of the learner's products are assessed through holistic scoring. Several assessors should review to establish a consensus of standards or to ensure greater reliability—usually with the use of a rubric.

Reliability: Getting the same response or results across multiple occurrences or multiple judges. When the same results occur repeatedly, the measure is considered reliable. In other words, an instrument should yield similar results over time with similar populations in similar circumstances. If it does not, the measure is not reliable.

Rubric Scoring: Scores specific traits, skills, behavior formats, processes, or products.

Standard Deviation: The measure of the extent to which scores in a distribution, on the average, deviate from their mean. One step in the calculation of the standard deviation is to subtract each score from the mean. The resulting deviation scores are then squared and entered into a formula to yield the standard deviation. The standard deviation forms the basis for various types of standard scores, such as Z scores, T scores, and Stanine scores. In the Normal Curve 0.13 percentile is 3 standard deviations below the mean; 2.28 percentile is 2 standard deviations below the mean; 15.87 percentile is 1 standard deviation below the mean; 50 percentile is at the mean; 84.13 percentile is 1 standard deviation above the mean; 97.92 is 2 standard deviations above the mean; 99.87 is 3 standard deviations above the mean.

Test: A measure of skill, capacity, or knowledge.

> **Achievement Test:** A standardized test designed to measure amount of knowledge or skills the learner has obtained from instruction.

> **Aptitude Test:** A test intended to measure the test-taker's ability to learn; it is given before instruction occurs.

> **Criterion-Referenced Test:** Performance is compared to an expected level of mastery in a content rather than to other students' scores.

Norm-Referenced Test: The test compares the test-taker's score to the group used to norm the test.

Standardized Test: An objective test given and scored by guidelines in a manual to administer and score the test.

Validity: Measuring what you intended to measure. In other words, the instrument measures the desired performance and appropriate conclusions can be made from the results. The assessment accurately reflects the learning it was designed to measure. (To measure writing, you would want to use a "valid" measure such as writing samples rather than multiple-choice, which would not be as valid.)

Scoring Guide for Divergent Thinking and Pupil Assessment Matrix for Williams Creativity Assessment Packet

In Chapter 3 of the text, a description of The Williams Creativity Assessment Packet is provided. In this appendix, there is a guide for scoring the Test of Divergent Thinking. After the test taker transforms shapes into pictures, the scoring of those transformations occurs in five categories. They are fluency, flexibility, originality, elaboration, and titles. The Test of Divergent Feeling is scored using a template. The Williams Scale, which is a teacher or parent rating scale, is scored using the guide on the questionnaire itself. Questions are answered and rated according to *always* (2 points), *sometimes* (1 point), or *seldom* (0 points). Once scores have been obtained for the Divergent Thinking, Divergent Feeling, and the Parent Rating Scale, the raw scores are highlighted on the Pupil Assessment Matrix to determine their relationship to the mean score and standard deviation above or below the mean. The description of the scoring procedures for the Test of Divergent Thinking and the Pupil Assessment Matrix follows.

4

Scoring Instructions

Scoring for each of the three instruments of the packet will be discussed separately.

Test of Divergent Thinking

All four cognitive factors of divergent thinking strongly correlated with the creative process (right brain visual perspective skill) are measured along with a fifth score vocabulary synthesis (left brain verbal skill). Five raw scores are obtained. They include Fluency (F_L), Flexibility (F_X), Originality (O), Elaboration (E), and Title (T).

FLUENCY

Quantity of production by count of frames attempted regardless of what was done in each.

Rationale: Creative people are productive, hence obtain higher fluency.

1 to 12 points possible (one point per frame).

FLEXIBILITY

Number of times the picture shifts from *category of first frame* across the five possible categories listed below:

Living (L)—person, face, flower, tree, animal, etc.

Mechanical (M)—boat, spaceship, bicycle, car, tool, toy, equipment, etc.

Symbol (S)—letter, number, name, flag, or something expressing a meaning, etc.

View (V)—city, highway, ocean, mountains, yard, park, etc.

Utility (U)—house, clothing, food, furniture, etc. (See illustrations on next page.)

Rationale: Creative people will shift often rather than rigidly hanging on to one way or one category. Not fixed but flexible.

1 to 11 points depending upon the *number of times the picture category shifts after the initial category.*

ORIGINALITY

Where person works on drawing. Each frame has a closed part created by the stimulus line or form shown. This part acts as a restriction to a less creative person. Originality is highest for those who draw in and around the form or restricted part.

11

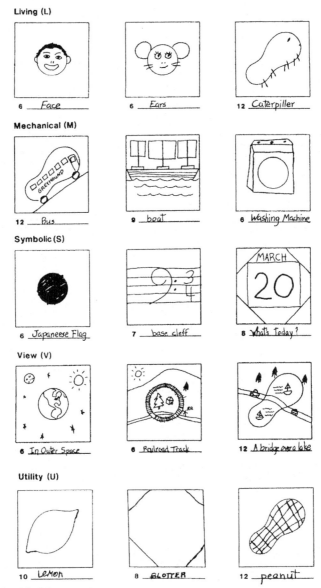

Figure 2. Examples of flexibility categories.

12

Rationale: Less creative people are blocked by the closed portion and will avoid it. More creative people will
              inside the closed part and will be structured from outside. Highly creative people will create a synt
              and not be structured nor blocked by any closed portion.

1 point—draw *outside closure* only. See Sample 1.

2 points—draw *inside closure* only. See Sample 2.

3 points—draw *both inside-outside closure* (synthesis). See Sample 3.

These points per frame times number of frames attempted equals total Originality (O) raw score points.

2 <u>Funny Looking Clown</u>   5 <u>A Child's Block</u>   4 <u>Sunny Marooned Island</u>

SAMPLE 1:   SAMPLE 2:   SAMPLE 3:
   1 Point   2 Points   3 Points
   (outside closure)   (inside closure)   (inside/outside
                                                    closure synthesis)

Figure 3. Examples of originality categories.

ELABORATION

Where details are placed making picture asymmetrical.

0 points—symmetrical both inside and outside closed space. See Sample 1. (next page)

1 point—asymmetrical *outside* closure. See Sample 2.

2 points—asymmetrical *inside* closure. See Sample 3.

3 points—asymmetrical throughout with off-sided details both inside and outside closure. See Sample 4.

These points per frame times number of frames attempted equals total Elaboration (E) raw score points.

TITLES

Length and complexity of vocabulary usage.

0 points—No titles given.

1 point—Simple title without modifier. (See completed test sample, Form A, frames 2, 4, 8, 10 & 12.)

2 points—Name with descriptive modifier. (See completed test sample, Form A, frames 5, 9 & 11.)

13

Pupil Assessment Matrix

Student's Name_____ Date _____

Age_____ Grade_____ Sex_____

ASSESSMENTS   RANGES OF WEIGHTED RAW SCORES

	Standard Deviations Below		-MEAN-		Standard Deviations Above		
	1.0	.5	0	.5	1.0	1.5	2.0
CREATIVE THINKING							
Total Score	60-69	70-79	80-89	90-99	100-110	111-120	121 +
Fluency	7		8-10		11		12
Flexibility	4	5	6-7	8	9	10	11
Originality	16-18	19-21	22-25	26-27	28-30	31-32	33 +
Elaboration	7-9	10-13	14-17	18-21	22-25	26-30	31 +
Title	17-19	20-22	23-25	26-28	29-31	32-33	34 +
CREATIVE FEELING							
Total Score	44-50	51-58	59-65	66-72	73-80	81-88	89 +
Curiosity	10-12	13-14	15-17	18-19	20-21	22-23	24
Imagination	12	13-14	15-17	18-19	20-21	22	23
Complexity	8-10	11-12	13-15	16-18	19-20	22	22
Risk-Taking	9-11	12-13	14-15	16-18	19-20	21-22	23
PARENT/TEACHER RATINGS	24-33	34-43	44-51	52-59	60-69	70-79	80 +

Place an "x" in the appropriate box indicating a possible range of scores for the weighted raw score obtained by a tested pupil's total and sub-factor scores. Connect the "x's" with a line forming a profile of the pupil's performance as compared to at, above, or below the mean average score obtained by groups of other tested pupils. As a general rule of thumb, one standard deviation above the mean (average) represents a score at around the 83rd percentile, while one standard deviation below is at about the 17th percentile. Two standard deviations above is at about the 96th percentile.

Appendix C

Portfolio Evaluation
Samples

Chapter 4 of the text addresses the use of performance-based assessment procedures to assess samples of student work. Rubrics may be used to evaluate a student's performance on a portfolio entry or project. These two samples might be used with a written or visual project submitted by a student for a course project in any academic content or area of interest. The samples demonstrate a variety of ways a project or sample from a portfolio maight be evaluated—quantifying what would otherwise be subjective.

PORTFOLIO RUBRIC

Criteria for Scoring

Student:_____Date:_____Content:_____

Teacher, peer, or self evaluation may be provided for written and visual products presented in this portfolio of student work.

	Exemplary 3 points	Satisfactory 2 points	Needs Consideration 1 point	Total Points
WRITTEN PRODUCT				
Evidence of Understanding				
Accuracy				
Mechanics				
Organization				
VISUAL PRODUCT				
Visual Appeal				
Creativity				
Complete				

Points obtained _____ /21   Total Points = _____%

PORTFOLIO RUBRIC

Criteria for Scoring: Weighted

Student:_____Date:_____Content:_____

	Indicators	4	2	0	Total points
WRITTEN PRODUCT					
Evidence of Understanding	Concepts clearly stated Organized flow	Advanced level	Basic level	Unclear	__x3 (12)
Accuracy	Spelling Punctuation	0 errors	1-4 errors	5-8 errors	__x4 (16)
Mechanics	Sentence structure Grammar	0 errors	1-4 errors	5-8 errors	__x5 (20)
Organization Neatness	Paragraph Opening, supporting detail, closing Connectedness	Advanced level	Basic level	Incorrect	__x6 (24)
Presentation	Legibility Use of space	Advanced level	Basic level	Incorrect	__x7 (28)
90–100 A 80–89 B 70–79 C 60–69 D				Final Points _____ Final Grade_____	

Appendix D

Star Transformation and Other Enrichment Activities for Primary Students

In Chapter 5 a sample lesson, according to the *CREATE* Model, is presented (page 52). In the lesson students are required to transform shapes into pictures as evidence of creative production. The following star shape is used with that lesson, Lesson 1 in the unit "It's all about Bears." Additional lessons and transformation shapes are included here. The children who provide multiple and unique ideas during these lessons may be considered for additional screening and assessment in the area of creative potential.

Use the star in the center of the page to create something new. Try to think of a way to use the star in a picture that will be different from everyone else's.

Lesson 2—
A Bear's Journey

Objective: Students will use creative process while listening, making predictions, and creating original products.

Fluency: Students will brainstorm places they might like to go.

Flexibility: Teacher will list the ideas in categories (e.g., places in town, places within the United States, places in other countries, etc.).

Students will hear following story:

Bear Lee loved to take trips. It didn't matter if they were short trips, like to see Mommaw and Pawpaw, who lived just across town, or if they were traveling trips, like going on a camping and fishing trip to a spring-fed river with dad. He simply loved to travel.

Maybe it was his love for travel that made him dream of all the places he might like to go. He thought about taking a trip to (**8, 16, 20, 21**). In his thoughts, he would also drift away to places like the Grand Canyon in Arizona, the Eiffel Tower in Paris, France, or Niagara Falls of Ontario, Canada.

One night, as Bear Lee ate supper with his family, he announced his desire to travel. To his surprise, his mom and dad said, "Sure, someday you might travel to (**1, 5, 12, 18**)." Later that evening, in his room, he began to pack. He packed (**2, 4, 11, 19**). And later that night, his journey began.

As if he were being swept away on a magic carpet, he flew very swiftly. He suddenly realized he was flying in a (**3, 6, 7, 10**). "Oh my. Oh my," he said, "I'm flying in a time machine." As he went back, back, back in time, he landed at the first of the Ancient Wonders of the World.

He was at the Pyramid of Giza—the only remaining wonder of the seven ancient wonders. Oh what a sight, this great pyramid of Egypt.

He was then suddenly swept away to his next stop at the Hanging Gardens of Babylon, near our now-a-day Baghdad, Iraq. Just as he was inhaling the sweet smells of all the gardens, which reminded him of honey, off he went again.

This time he landed in Greece, where he saw the Statute of Zeus, which was used in the Olympic games of Ancient Greece. While standing by this monument, he thought, "Hmmm, I wonder (**13, 14, 17, 25**)." Just as he was about to touch the HUGE statute, he was whisked away to Turkey.

In Turkey, he saw the Temple of Artemis at Ephesus and the Mausoleum, which was a gigantic monument for dead kings—much like the great pyramids of Egypt.

In a blink, he found himself at the Colossus of Rhodes, another HUGE statue like our Statue of Liberty.

His final stop was the Lighthouse of Alexandria, in Egypt. He knew it used to guide ships into the harbor.

When his time machine landed in his back yard, Bear Lee felt the jolt. He slowly opened his eyes and realized the jolt was really (**22, 23, 24**) his mom shaking him. He had fallen asleep while packing for his trip and dreamed about the Seven Ancient Wonders. What a nice dream! It which made him really anxious for his next real trip to travel and see something new and exciting.

Originality: Students will be given a page with a pyramid shape to transform into something new and different.

Elaboration: Each student will write a brief story about his/her picture.

Use the pyramid in the center of the page to create something new. Try to think of a way to use the pyramid in a picture that will be different from everyone else's.

Lesson 3—
Where is Math?

Objective: Students will use creative process while listening, making predictions, and creating original products.

Fluency: Students will brainstorm things they know about math.

Flexibility: Teacher will list the ideas in categories (e.g., a list of numbers, things you can do with math, like add, subtract, etc.). Be sure to call attention to the different paths, like "it rhymes with bath."

Students will hear the following story:

Bear Lee was such a smart little bear, and he just loved doing math. He really liked counting. In fact, one day he counted all of his (**4, 8, 11, 19**). He liked to add numbers together; he liked to take numbers away, or subtract. He even liked to multiply and divide numbers.

He liked math so-o-o-o much that one day, while he was playing by his favorite pond in the woods, he found a turtle—and he named him "Math." They were pretty good buddies for a little while, until Bear Lee got side-tracked looking closely at some bugs on a leaf, and Math wondered off back down to the pond.

Well, when Bear Lee realized Math was gone, the search was on. He looked (**5, 17, 20, 23, 9, 21, 22**). Bear Lee came upon his dad, who was mowing the lawn. And he asked, "Dad, where is Math?" His dad said, "Well son, math is at the bank where I work during the day. You see, we use math to balance all the accounts and calculate interest. We simply couldn't do without math."

The next day, Bear Lee went to the bank with his dad, but he could not find Math. When he got home, he asked his mom,

"Mom, where is Math?" She said, "Well, math is in the kitchen when your dad and I fix dinner. We use math to measure out the ingredients in the food we eat." Bear Lee ran to the kitchen. He looked (**2, 6, 12, 16**), but he did not find Math.

The next day, Bear Lee went to school. He asked his teacher, Mrs. Wright Bear, "Where is Math?" Mrs. Wright told him that math was right there in the classroom. She explained that math helped all boys and girls learn to count and calculate, which would make them better students always. Bear Lee got excited and started looking (**1, 3 14, 18**). But still he found no Math.

It wasn't until that afternoon that Bear Lee went back to the pond, sad that Math had not been in any of the places he had been told. When he got there, sitting by the edge of the pond, there was Math. They played and played until it was time for Bear Lee to go home following the call of his parents to come to dinner.

Originality: Students will create a picture using the number in the center of the page.

Elaboration: Students will give their picture a title.

Use the number 8 in the center of the page to create something new. Try to think of a way to use the number 8 in a picture that will be different from everyone else's.

Lesson 4—
Nice Things to Say

Objective: Students will use creative process while listening, making predictions, and creating original products.

Fluency: Students will brainstorm nice things to say and do.

Flexibility: Teacher will list the ideas in categories (e.g., compliments, nice things to say on the playground, different situations to say "excuse me," etc.). Call attention to the different paths, like the nice things to say if you spill soup on a giraffe.

Students will hear the following story:

It was a cool fall day and the leaves were playing in the cool fall air. Bear Lee was walking home from school with his bear friends when all of a sudden one of them, Climbing Bear, let out the biggest belch ever heard by bear ears. Bear Lee was quit embarrassed and explained that it is proper to say, "Excuse me" when we have an accidental belch.

Bear Lee explained that he knew all about nice things to say and do since his Pawpaw shared the manner card with him when he was a little bitty bear. He explained further that the manner card was an Ace of Spades card out of the deck of playing cards, and that when he was a little bear and not so full of nice things to say, his Pawpaw would hold up the ace to remind him when it was polite for him to say or do something nice.

The next day on the playground, his same friend pushed and broke right up to the front of the lunch line. Bear Lee didn't have an ace card, so he said, "Climbing Bear, instead of pawing and climbing to the front of the line, it would be better if you (**4, 8, 11, 19**).

Later that same day, at recess, Climbing Bear wanted the swing first, so he shoved a little bear cub in kindergarten out of the way.

Bear Lee said, "Climbing, the polite thing to say or do is (**9, 21, 22**)."

When it was time to go back to class and do work, Furry dropped her pencil on the floor and it rolled right under Climbing's desk. Instead of picking it up, Climbing said, "(**2, 6, 12, 16**)."

The next day, Bear Lee brought an ace card, and every time Climbing needed to be reminded to say or do something polite, Bear Lee would show him the card. That day, Climbing remembered to say, "Thank you," "You're welcome," "You go first," and "Excuse me."

Originality: Students will create a picture using the "ace of spades" in the center of the page.

Elaboration: Students will give their picture a title.

Use the spade in the center of the page to create something new. Try to think of a way to use the spade in a picture that will be different from everyone else's.

Lesson 5—
Creative Things to Do
on a Rainy Day

Objective: Students will use creative process while listening, making predictions, and creating original products.

Fluency: Students will brainstorm things to do on a rainy day.

Flexibility: Teacher will list the ideas in categories (e.g., games you can play, things to watch on TV, things you can make). Call attention to the different paths, like "get in a boat and sail away to a sunny place."

Students will hear following story:

Saturday was always Bear Lee's favorite day. It was the day he got to do all kinds of fun things he wished to do. There was no homework to do and generally no place in particular he had to go with his folks. So, most Saturdays Lee would play outside. While he was outside, he would (**4, 8, 11, 19, 5, 17**).

But once in a while on Saturday, it would rain. When he would awake on a rainy Saturday, his first thought was almost always, "Now, this just about messes up everything."

On one particular rainy Saturday, during breakfast, he asked his mom, "Mom, what can I do today since it's raining and I can't go outside and play?" His mom said he could (**20, 23, 9, 21**). But he didn't like any of those ideas.

Next, he asked his dad, "Dad, what can I do today since it's raining outside?" His dad said, "(**22, 2, 6, 12**)." But he didn't like any of those ideas either.

Up into his room he went, and he started looking for some paper, glue, markers, and scissors. He decided he would start his day by making a (**1, 3, 16**). Oh my, this was great fun!

After a while he was ready to do something else. So, he decided he would get out some of his favorite inside toys and play (**14, 18, 7**). He played and played and played.

Just then, mom called him for lunch. "But it couldn't be time for lunch," he thought, "I just finished breakfast." Sure enough a long time had passed, but he was having so much fun playing rainy day things, he hadn't noticed his empty tummy.

After lunch, his dad asked him if he wanted to play (**10, 13, 15**). So, he and dad played a game of checkers and a game of chess.

Mom asked him if he wanted to make some cookies and read a mystery story. Well, by the time all that was done, it was time to have dinner, take a bath, say his prayers, and go to sleep. As he was drifting off to sleep, he thought, "You know, rainy Saturdays can be pretty bright after all."

Originality: Take the sun shape and transform it by using it in a picture of something different, unique, and unusual.

Elaboration: Give it a name.

Use the sun in the center of the page to create something new. Try to think of a way to use the sun in a picture that will be different from everyone else's.

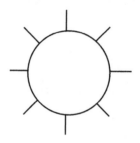

Lesson 6—
Bears Wonder, "What If."

Objective: Students will use creative process while listening, making predictions, and creating original products.

Fluency: Students will answer following questions:

WHAT IF A TOAD FROG LIVED
IN YOUR DRESSER DRAWER?

WHAT IF ALL CLOUDS WERE PURPLE?

WHAT IF YOU LIVED UNDER WATER?

WHAT IF CARS ONLY WENT BACKWARDS?

WHAT IF ALL HOUSES WERE UNDERGROUND?

WHAT IF OUR EARS WERE AT THE
ENDS OF OUR FINGERS?

WHAT IF ALL PICTURES WERE HUNG UPSIDE DOWN?

Flexibility: Have kids create questions of their own.

Students will hear following story:

Bear Lee was just amazed at things around him; he loved to look at things up close, like (**4, 8, 11, 19**). When he went outside to play or he was playing in his room, he was always questioning, "I wonder what would happen if (**5, 17, 20, 23**)."

One day, while he was playing outside, he got really intrigued by the plants all around him. He noticed that there were all kinds of different grass, and there were all kinds of different flowers, like (**2, 6, 12**). So Bear Lee began to wonder, "Hmmm, I wonder what plants need to grow. I wonder if seeds from plants can grow without soil. I wonder if they must have water and light."

How could we help him find out (**22, 23, 24**)?

So, Bear Lee set up the experiment to see "what if."

The next day, Bear Lee was watching his mom and dad cook in the kitchen. As they were preparing the honey cakes and the honey sauce, he wondered, "Hmmm, I wonder if fire could burn without oxygen (or air). What do you think (**1, 3, 14, 18**)? He asked his mom and dad how he could find out. His dad said they could take a candle, light it, and put a jar around it to see if it would continue to burn without any air.

So, Bear Lee and his dad set up an experiment to find out "what if."

Following lunch, he went back outside and noticed different kinds of leaves. He thought maybe they had come off different kinds of trees. like (**7, 9, 10, 21**). He wondered, "What if I take each of the different kinds of leaves and put them between two sheets of paper? Then, what if I rubbed a crayon on the top paper? Would the print of the leaf come off on the paper? Would the print of the different kinds of leaves look different?

So Bear Lee set up an experiment.

What else might we find out "what if" (**13, 15**)?

Originality: Students will create a picture with the clover leaf.

Elaboration: Once finished, have each child add some additional detail.

Use the clover in the center of the page to create something new. Try to think of a way to use the clover in a picture that will be different from everyone else's.

An Activity Book
for Students and Teachers
of Gifted Education

CHAPTER 1:
History of Assessing and Identifying Giftedness

Questions:

After reading chapter 1, do you feel the use of IQ to determine giftedness is appropriate for identifying giftedness with the students at your school? Why or why not?

_____

_____

_____

_____

What about the use of non-traditional measures to determine giftedness? What are some possible uses at your school?

_____

_____

_____

_____

Field Activity:

Talk to a variety of school administrators and school counselors from a variety of schools (approximately 4 schools). Ask him and/or her if IQ is used to determine giftedness at their school? Ask if he/she agrees with the use (or not) of an IQ assessment to guide decisions about placement of children in the program for gifted, talented, and creative students. Compare their answers. Which of their beliefs or guiding principles do you agree with or not? Why or why not?

_____

_____

_____

Scenario:

You have just been called to the principal's office. When you get there, concerned parents are waiting. The principal explains that the parents have a child, who has been nominated by his second grade classroom teacher to be "tested" for the TAG (Talented and Gifted) Program. She explains further that the parents are concerned about their child taking an IQ test. They want to know what it means to assess IQ. How will you address their concerns? And will you recommend that their child be tested with an IQ assessment instrument?

_____

_____

_____

_____

Scenario:

A classroom teacher meets you in the hall at lunch and asks you about the difference between the use of tests (traditional methods) and samples of students' work (nontraditional) to determine giftedness. How would you give a concise and accurate explanation for the importance of using both?

_____

_____

_____

_____

_____

_____

_____

CHAPTER 2
Defining Assessment of Giftedness

Questions:

What did Rachel Carson, Jonas Salk, Thomas Jefferson, and Mary Bethune contribute to society? How do we know they were gifted?

_____

_____

_____

_____

_____

_____

Activity:

Go to your state's Web site. Look up the rules, regulations, guidelines, or legislation for gifted education. What is the definition your state uses for giftedness? How is your state's definition for giftedness like or different from Sidney Marland's definition in his address to Congress?

_____

_____

_____

_____

_____

_____

_____

Scenario:

You have just been asked to speak at the next school board meeting. The superintendent has asked you to explain the definition for giftedness according to state policy and the identification process expected by the state. Prepare your presentation in outline form here. (Create a power point, handbook, or handouts of your choice for the school board presentation. Present this to your class peers.)

_____

_____

_____

_____

_____

_____

Scenario:

You have just received a phone call from a parent. She says she is upset to see an article in the paper showing the TAG (Talented and Gifted) class at the Project Fair. She says that all kids are gifted and that to have a picture in the paper of a group called the gifted is promoting elitism. She asks you bluntly, "Why should those kids be identified and provided something different from the other kids?" How would you respond?

_____

_____

_____

_____

_____

_____

CHAPTER 3
Assessment Procedures and Instruments

Activity:

Choose four of the cognitive reasoning assessment instruments to examine further. Go to the Mental Measurement Yearbook www.mentalmeasurement.com to retrieve information about reliability and validity of the instrument, the cost, and a description of the assessment instrument. Which of the tests you reviewed do you think might be useful with the students at your school. Why? Which ones would not seemingly be appropriate for students at your school? Why not?

Test _____

_____

_____

Test _____

_____

_____

Test _____

_____

_____

Test _____

_____

_____

Field Activity:

Choose any two of the creativity measures. Administer both of them to the same child at two different times. (If you choose questionnaires to be completed by parents or teachers, give them to different adults to be completed on behalf of the same child.) Compare the results in terms of percentiles. How do they compare? Which one would you prefer using with the students at your school? Why?

_____

_____

_____

_____

_____

_____

Scenario:

You have just received an email from a school board member. He writes that he has just been reading a brochure about the TAG (Talented and Gifted) Program, which he picked up from the administrative office earlier in the week. He tells you he doesn't understand the need to assess cognitive, creative, and leadership performance to determine giftedness. How do you answer him? Email me your response as if I am the board member. We will create a dialog where I may play the devil's advocate, so be ready to defend your answer. Prepare your remarks below.

_____

_____

_____

_____

CHAPTER 4
Identifying Giftedness among Subpopulations

Question:

How can you justify using different assessment instruments with minority students? Or can you?

_____

_____

_____

_____

_____

Activity:

Review the Naglieri Nonverbal Ability Text and the Raven's Progressive Matrices. Compare the two tests for reliability, validity, procedure for administering, and scoring. How are they alike or different? Would you recommend the use of one above the other? Which one? Why?

_____

_____

_____

_____

_____

Scenario:

You have just been called to interview for a position you've applied for in gifted education at an isolated rural school. The school is in a community at a very low socio-economic level.

During your interview with the superintendent, he tells you they only identify approximately 2% of their student body as gifted even though the state funds 5%. He expresses concern to you regarding the underrepresentation of students in the program for gifted children. He explains that the traditional use of standardized achievement tests and IQ seems to be an inhibitor since the students there do not score well. He asks you if you think changes could be made in the identification procedure. (At this point, you know that your response may impact you getting the job.) How would you answer? What would you promise?

_____

_____

_____

_____

Scenario:

You have just become the coordinator or administrator of the program for gifted children at a school district 30 miles from your home. It is a mining community where mines have closed, and the population is generally very poor. The townspeople are new to you. The superintendent suggests that you attend the community meeting and address the low representation of low-socio-economic children in TAG. How will you address this issue with the people of this community? Outline your comments here.

_____

_____

_____

_____

_____

CHAPTER 5
Discovering Potential in the Primary Grades

Question:

Should giftedness be identified among preschool or primary students? Justify your answer.

_____

_____

_____

_____

_____

Activity:

Using the CREATE Model, create a lesson plan for primary students that includes any or all of the components: creative process, react and interact, enhance knowledge, associative properties, thinking skills, and evaluate students' progress.

Lesson Plan

_____

_____

_____

_____

_____

_____

_____

_____

_____

Activity:

Document the progress of one class for one month using lessons that encourage creative process and production. What pattern do you see emerge? Are there particular students who almost always have the most marks for fluency of ideas or originality? What does this mean?

_____

_____

_____

_____

_____

_____

Scenario:

You, as a facilitator of gifted children, have just been called into the principal's office. When you arrive you find the kindergarten teacher, with whom you have been teaming. She is upset. She claims that she is too busy to stay in the classroom when you come in to do enrichment teaching—that she could be grading papers, putting up bulletin boards, or running off worksheets while you are there. She goes on to say that she doesn't feel qualified to mark or document students' creative performance on a chart while you are teaching. Finally, she says she simply doesn't understand why you are trying to take away her break. How do you respond to each concern?

_____

_____

_____

_____

_____

_____

CHAPTER 6
Cooperation with Classroom Teachers

Activity:

Create six questions regarding the definition of giftedness, identifying giftedness, and serving giftedness. Interview six classroom teachers at any level. Report their responses to your interview questions. What did you learn about these classroom teachers' knowledge about giftedness? How can you use their responses to help you better educate teachers at your school about assessing, identifying, and serving gifted kids?

_____

_____

_____

_____

_____

_____

_____

Activity:

Make a list of additional ways you might bridge the gap between classroom teachers and the facilitator of gifted children to make the identification process a cooperative one.

_____

_____

_____

_____

_____

_____

Scenario:

It is the end of September. You send out a letter to all teachers at your school. The letter states that you are welcoming nominations of students for assessment into the TAG Program. One of the 2nd grade teachers tells you that she has a child in her classroom, who is reading at the 4th grade level, exhibiting exceptional creative problem solving skills, has an advanced vocabulary, and is intellectually superior to classmates. BUT she does not believe in identifying students for giftedness. What do you say? Also, what do you do that might reinforce a cooperative spirit?

_____

_____

_____

_____

_____

Scenario:

The principal of the same school asks you to come to the first faculty meeting to talk about the assessment procedure toward identifying and serving the TAG students. You know you have at least one teacher who does not agree with the identification of giftedness. You suspect there are others with the same perception. Describe how you will address (1) the need to assess giftedness, (2) team teaching and documentation of potential, and 3) cooperative efforts to serve gifted students' learning needs.

_____

_____

_____

_____

_____

CHAPTER 7
Putting it all Together

Questions:

Why is it important to use percentiles when documenting scores on a profile sheet?

_____

_____

_____

_____

_____

_____

_____

How would you go about choosing and training an identification committee concerning the assessment instruments you use for identifying giftedness, the interpretation of scores, and the definition of giftedness?

_____

_____

_____

_____

_____

_____

_____

Scenario:

You are in charge of an identification committee meeting. The committee is reviewing the scores of a child who has an extremely high cognitive abilities score (e.g., IQ of 145), an average score on the creativity assessment, and very poor grades. The committee announces that they have no idea what to recommend regarding the placement of the child. How do you advise them? How do you feel about the placement of this child? Why?

_____

_____

_____

_____

_____

_____

_____

Scenario:

You are called by the president of the Rotary Club and invited to come and talk about identification of gifted, talented, and creative children. Prepare a presentation you can do in about 15 minutes. Include in this presentation a definition for giftedness, the assessment process, and how the definition matches the procedure. Include information about how the process is fair and nondiscriminatory.

_____

_____

_____

_____

_____

_____

Most Commonly Asked Questions by Educators of Gifted Kids and Administrators of Programs for the Gifted

Question: Should I use an IQ test to determine giftedness?

Answer: Sure, use a cognitive performance test—a measure of abstract reasoning, problem solving, memory, etc. such as the Henmon-Nelson Test of Mental Ability, Kaufman Brief Intelligence Test, Slosson Intelligence Test. But IQ tests should be used as one part of the whole assessment picture. Use IQ test scores in conjunction with other measures.

Consider the following: Suppose a 5-year-old who exhibits characteristics of intellectual giftedness (e.g., vast and advanced vocabulary, reads early, learns rapidly, advanced problem solving ability, etc.) has been nominated for TAG Program services and an IQ test is one standard for assessing the gifted at your school. If that child scores 135 on an IQ test, it is no fluke. Consider this IQ test score as one good piece of evidence needed to confirm the child's giftedness.

But, beware! If a child exhibits characteristics of creative and intellectual giftedness, and cognitive and creative performance measures are given but test scores are just average, NEVER DISREGARD THE OBSERVATIONAL DATA. Continue to observe the child and document the child's gifts using nontraditional or performance-based measures (portfolio, creative products, stories, documentation of problem solutions, and the like). Use the data in the case study for review by the committee that assists you with decisions about students' placement in the program for the gifted.

Question: Can I use an IQ test with very young children?

Answer: Some IQ tests have been normed with children from birth. However, these are not very reliable assessments. More reliable assessments for verbal and abstract thinking skills begin about age 4. (See Chapter 3 for specific examples.)

Question: How should traditional and non-traditional assessments be used simultaneously?

Answer: Many times state guidelines will mandate the number of objective and subjective measures required in order to meet state standards. When no guidelines exist, at least three measures of each is a good rule of thumb. For example, you might use a standardized cognitive performance test (IQ test), a standardized creativity assessment, and/or a standardized achievement measure combined with portfolio samples of creative writing, projects, and teacher observational checklists. Add to that parent questionnaires and/or rating scales for motivation, creativity, and leadership, and you have a pretty thorough mix of traditional and performance-based assessment measures to compile the case study for review by the identification/selection committee.

Question: Do I really need an identification committee to help make decisions about the placement of children in the program for gifted and talented students?

Answer: Yes! And for a number of reasons. First, simply because it can help in making sound decisions. When multiple professionals review the student profile data, there may be some piece of evidence that a committee member sees that others had not considered. For example, if writing samples from student portfolios are presented and an English teacher is a member of the committee, that person's expertise is valuable to assist other members in seeing potential of a student who might otherwise be overlooked.

But for another reason, it is sometimes a good thing in parent conferences to create confidence that no teacher bias affected the placement decision—no one person reviewed student scores and made a judgment, but rather an anonymous review was conducted by multiple professionals.

Finally, many states mandate the use of a committee to make decisions about the placement of children into programs for the gifted.

You want to have a committee who will review the case studies in a condensed form (see Chapter 4 for sample profile sheets). The committee members should be willing to spend some time after school a few times per academic year to review student profiles.

Question: Who chooses or selects the Identification Committee? If I do, whom do I ask? What if they turn down my request?

Answer: Typically, the program coordinator or administrator is responsible for asking colleagues to serve as members of the Identification Committee. It is a good idea to ask a variety of educators at various levels to serve. For example, you might ask one principal, one counselor, a couple of teachers from the primary levels, some from the middle level, and some from the high school level. There is no "right" number. However, I suggest having no more than 10 on the committee.

If someone wishes not to serve on the committee, just ask someone else. You certainly don't want unwilling participants making decisions about which children should be served.

Question: If only 3–5% of the population is truly gifted, how do I ensure that I place the "right" kids—the ones that are "truly gifted"?

Answer: Remember, Marland's 1971 definition included a percentage of 3–5%. And most states that mandate gifted education provide funding for approximately 5% of the total school population. Still, there is no magic in this number. Some researchers, Renzulli, for example, advocate programs for about 20% of the student population (see Chapter 7 for Web sites about Talent Pools).

There are many factors to consider when educators and administrators make decisions and policies about the numbers of students that should be identified as gifted and placed in programs for gifted children. So, let's begin to answer the original question with some additional questions: Does your state mandate a percentage of students for placement? If so, you should calculate the numbers this would entail. For example, at 5%, if your school contains 250 students, you'll be required to identify 13 students. Once students are nominated, testing is completed, collection of data is final, and the Identification Committee is assembled, you may announce that the program only has 3 available slots since you presently serve 10 students. Thus, the profile sheets may be ranked. Once the committee has agreed (by majority) on the top three profiles, those students would be placed.

If you are not bound by state mandates, rules, or regulations to a maximum number of students, the placement may be handled according to the following: When students are nominated for placement and each one has been tested, profiles are condensed into a data sheet, and the Identification Committee meets, you might have the forms numbered. Each member reviews the profile sheet and rates the placement "yes," "no," or "I need more evidence." If the majority of the committee agrees on placement, then the child is placed in the program. If the majority agrees that the candidate appears to be average and the regular classroom is the best placement for the child, then it is so. If the majority feels the evidence doesn't persuade them one way or the other, then this collection of evidence may continue (more samples of the students' work, other tests may be given, etc.) More students will likely be included in the program by using this method.

Back to the hard question: How do we ensure the "truly gifted" will be placed? There is NO definitive means to accurately identify every bright and creative child in the program. Some underachievers will go unnoticed. Some exceptionally creative kids may not meet other criteria, such as exceptional cognitive performance assessment scores, achievement, or motivation. And perhaps not every bright and creative child needs the program's services. We simply must do the BEST WE CAN DO with the available human and capital resources.

Index

CPSIA information can be obtained
at www.ICGtesting.com
Printed in the USA
BVOW11s2354260516

449493BV00008B/125/P